ID0984238

ATLA BIBLIOGRAPHY SERIES
edited by Dr. Kenneth E. Rowe

RESEARCH IN RITUAL STUDIES:

a programmatic essay and bibliography

by
Ronald L. Grimes

ATLA Bibliography Series, No. 14

The American Theological
Library Association
and
The Scarecrow Press, Inc.
METUCHEN, N.J., & LONDON
1985

Z5118
R5
G75
1985

Library of Congress Cataloging in Publication Data

Grimes, Ronald L., 1943-
  Research in ritual studies.

  (ATLA bibliography series ; no. 14)
  Includes index.
  1. Rites and ceremonies--Bibliography.
2. Ritual--Bibliography. I. Title. II. Series.
Z5118.R5G75 1985 [GN473] 016.392   84-23474
ISBN 0-8108-1762-4

In memory of Victor W. Turner

1920-1983

CONTENTS

ACKNOWLEDGMENTS

For their assistance in helping prepare this bibliography my thanks to Roland Delattre, Volney Gay, Linda Hess, Ted Jennings, Aidan Kavanagh, Peter McLaren, Frank Manning, S. L. Scott; also to teaching assistants Jayne DeWeerd and Susan Dunlop.

EDITOR'S NOTE

The American Theological Library Association Bibliography series is designed to stimulate and encourage the preparation of reliable bibliographies and guides to the literature of religious studies in all of its scope and variety. Compilers are free to define their field, make their own selections, and work out internal organization as the unique demands of the subject require. We are pleased to publish Ronald L. Grimes' Research in Ritual Studies as number fourteen in our series.

Ronald L. Grimes is Associate Professor of Religion and Culture in the Wilfrid Laurier University, Waterloo, Ontario.

Kenneth E. Rowe
Series Editor

Drew University Library
Madison, New Jersey 07940

RESEARCH IN RITUAL STUDIES:
A PROGRAMMATIC ESSAY*

Because ritual studies comprise a newly consolidated field
within religious studies, a high degree of methodological and
bibliographical self-consciousness is necessary. And because
this subject's aspirations are interdisciplinary, it is obligated
to differentiate and relate its task to several other disciplines
such as liturgical theology, symbolic anthropology, art criticism, history of religions, and psychology of religion. Three
major goals of ritual studies are (1) to mediate between nor-
mative and descriptive, as well as textual and field-observa-
tional, methods; (2) to lay the groundwork for a coherent
taxonomy and theory that can account for the full range
of symbolic acts running from ritualization behavior in animals, through interaction ritual, to highly differentiated religious liturgies and civil ceremonies; and (3) to cultivate
the study of ritual in a manner that does not automatically
assume it to be a dependent variable.

With this agenda in mind, I collected over 1,600 English-
language items, most of them dating from 1960 to the present.
The data were from indexes, journals, card catalogs, bibliographies and correspondence with other scholars. My attempt
to classify these books and articles resulted in the following
outline:

1. Ritual Components
    1.1 Action (movement, dance, performance, mime,
         music, rhythm, gesture, play, work)

*Reprinted by permission from Religious Studies Review, 10/2
(April 1984), pp. 134-45.

1.2 Space (geography, environment, architecture, cosmology, shrines, sacred places)
1.3 Time (season, holiday, repetition, calendar)
1.4 Objects (masks, costumes, fetishes, icons, art)
1.5 Symbol, metaphor
1.6 Group (role, kinship, class, caste, family, hierarchy, ethnicity, acculturation)
1.7 Self (body, feeling, states of consciousness, gender)
1.8 Divine beings (gods, demons, spirits, animals, saints, ancestors)
1.9 Language (sound, song, poetry, word, story, myth)
1.10 Quality (e.g., color or shape), quantity, theme (e.g., evil)

2. Ritual Types
2.1 Rites of passage (couvade, birth, baptism, initiation, puberty, circumcision)
2.2 Marriage rites
2.3 Funerary rites (mortuary rites, death, mourning, unction, burial, cremation)
2.4 Festivals (celebrations, feasts, carnivals, contests, sports, games)
2.5 Pilgrimage (guests, processions, parades)
2.6 Purification (fasts, pollution, taboo, sin, confession)
2.7 Civil ceremony (royal rites, enthronement, legal ceremony, warfare)
2.8 Rituals of exchange (hunting, agricultural rites, ritual ecology, meals, food offerings, potlatch)
2.9 Sacrifice (decapitation, cannibalism, executions, violence, atonement)
2.10 worship (liturgy, prayer, sacraments)
2.11 Magic (fertility, divination, sorcery, oracles)
2.12 Healing rites (shamanism, psychedelics, exorcism, illness, therapy, dream incubation, possession)
2.13 Interaction rites (animal ritualization, habit, secular ritual)
2.14 Meditation rites (possession, conversion, trance)
2.15 Rites of inversion (rites of rebellion, clowning, joking, obscenity, revitalization rites)
2.16 Ritual drama (pageants, experimental rites, entertainment rites)

3. Ritual Descriptions (rites interpreted with primary reference to specific traditions, systems, periods, or geographical areas)

4. General Works in Various Field-Clusters
   4.1 Religious studies, theology, ethics, history of religions, liturgics
   4.2 Anthropology, ethnography, ethology, folklore
   4.3 Sociology, social psychology, political science
   4.4 Literature, literary criticism
   4.5 Philosophy
   4.6 History, classics
   4.7 Communications, kinesics, linguistics
   4.8 Psychology, medicine, biology, physics, genetics
   4.9 Education
   4.10 Theater, arts, music

Both the classification and sheer number of items present problems. For the purposes of this essay I can deal only with the classification problems by identifying a few illustrative ones. As for the list, I have chosen to reduce it programmatically. I do not try so much to reflect as to shape the field by singling out some works and skipping over others. My aim is to indicate topics and directions for fruitful research rather than identify representative examples of scholarship.

1. RITUAL COMPONENTS

In religious studies interpreting a ritual often begins with an invocation of terms suggesting that ritual is made up of components. These are imagined to be "building blocks" or "atoms." The result is a tangle of theoretical categories pulled from widely different thinkers. There is a little Kant-via-Eliade (sacred space and time), a bit of Aristotle-via-Burke (symbolic action), some Durkheim-via-Douglas (group), a little Freud-via-Erikson (self), and a growing dose of romantic Marxism-via-Turner (symbol). The categories are anything but systematic or mutually consistent, but they are the slots in which many works on ritual can be filed if one grants, as a bibliographer must, the categories stated or presupposed by scholars' titles and declared intentions.

The terms in parentheses within the outline are not sub-categories but associated key words, any one of which

could itself lead to an immense bibliography. In categories
where entries could have become numerous, for instance,
Language (1.9), Group (1.6), or Divine beings (1.8), I
have eliminated works not bearing directly on ritual. In
those promising few entries, for instance, Self (1.7) or
Quality (1.10), I have sometimes included works that may
only have implications for the study of ritual. Because I
believe components and types are badly in need of analysis, I have tried first to classify works in these two major
categories. Failing that, I entered them as descriptions or
general works--the former of more historical or phenomeno-
logical interest, the latter of methodological or theoretical
import. Consequently, the distinction between theoretical
and applied is rough at best. Many articles and books are
both, but because I avoided entering materials more than
once, I often had to make awkward classificatory choices.
The major justification for lumping together so many works
into such raggedly defined categories is to initiate serious
and sustained analysis of those categories. The development of a ritual criticism is an urgent research priority for
religious studies.

     Surprisingly little use has been made of the category
"ritual action" (1.1). Even though Mead and Burke, for
instance, have developed theories of social and verbal action, scholars seldom attend to specific ritual acts--gestures,
postures, and movements--and even less frequently make
overt actions central to the analysis of a rite. They are
far more likely to concentrate on the social context surround-
ing a rite, ritualists' commentary on it, or ritual texts that
dictate its scenarios. As a result, those that do focus on
ritual action tend to interpret it esthetically or formally--as
dance, drama, or play--in order to resist the reduction of
it to an epiphenomenon. Jennings' "On Ritual Knowledge"
is a good, short, theoretical statement on ritual action. On
ritual's relation to other sorts of action both the collection
edited by Schechner and Schuman and Schechner's Essays
on Performance Theory are examples of reliable, contemporary theorizing. Useful instances of applied research on
action and gesture are Thompson's African Art in Motion
and Saunders' work on mudras.

     The attention paid to ritual objects (1.4) and symbolic
qualities (1.10) is scant compared to that paid ritual space
(1.2) and time (1.3). Sam Gill's methodological inquiry into

color symbolism in Navajo ritual points the way to more sustained analyses of ritual qualities.

   Studies of ritual objects are typically photographic and
documentary, seldom interpretive. Exemplary exceptions are
Ludwig's historical study of New England gravestones and
Munn's volume on Walbiri iconography. The journal Studies
in the Anthropology of Visual Communication and the annual
Visible Religion (Kippenberg) make concerted efforts to ex-
pand our comprehension of the visual and tactile as primary
to religious practice.

   Smith's (1978) critique of Eliade's theory of sacred
space is essential reading. I can find no similar work on
ritual time, though Solberg's Redeem the Time: The Puritan Sabbath in Early America and Wigley's study of the Victorian Sunday illustrate the continued fruitfulness of analyzing set-aside times. Time as a theme is still very much wed
to the study of narrative and history.

   Symbol and metaphor (1.5) are in the process of being
rescued by Turner, Geertz, and their students from literary
criticism and linguistics for use in analyzing ritual. Symbol
theory, however, is not without its problems. In my estimation too little attention is paid to the differences between
symbolic action and symbolic language; even Turner and
Geertz are prone to treat symbols as if they are organized
analogously to language.

   Among some writers there is a notable tendency either
to restrict "symbol" to mean "symbolic object" or to overex-
tend the concept until every element in a rite is assumed,
on principle, to be symbolic. Fernandez is the most vocal
champion of metaphor; he insists that the difference between
symbol and metaphor in ritual is crucial. Even Turner has
responded by adding it to his theoretical repertoire in Dramas, Fields, and Metaphors. A useful summary of symbol
theory in anthropology can be found in Firth's Symbols:
Public and Private.

   An important theoretical challenge to the primacy of
symbolism in the study of ritual is developing. In Rethinking Symbolism Dan Sperber has argued the strongest case
for dispensing with a linguistic model in symbol theory; in
its place he suggests an "olfactory" one, which I think should

be taken more seriously than it has been in religious studies.
Staal's "The Meaninglessness of Ritual" (cf. Jarvie) is a different sort of critique, but one that also severely questions
the idea that rituals are composed of symbols-as-building-
blocks that "refer" to meanings.

The vast bulk of scholarship, implicitly following Durkheim, utilizes social categories (1.6) and ignores personal
ones (1.7). Social scientists and theologians alike define
ritual as a collective phenomenon, leaving its private mani-
festation open to easy, implicitly Freudian labeling as patho-
logical. Mary Douglas' "grid and group" theory of ritual
remains one of the most clearly articulated extensions of
Durkheim's work, and Gay's re-reading of Freud revises the
view that Freud considered ritual repressive. Other works
that point to new directions in research on ritual selfhood
are those by Smith-Rosenberg and Paige, both of which
touch upon the topic of ritual and gender. Feldstein's "The
Human Body as Rhythm and Symbol," although hymnic in
style, has interesting implications for understanding the
role of embodiment in enactment.

Though few scholars treat ritual as belonging to gods
(1.8) rather than religions, two that do so with some suc-
cess are Lodrick and Warner. Reading these, one wonders
what would happen if, for example, we imagined "the rites
of Yahweh," rather than the rites of Christianity or Judaism, to be the appropriate unit of study. Despite the work
of Eliade and Otto, in English-language articles and books
not much is made of the sacred or the holy as categories for
interpreting rituals except to use them as hedges against
reductionism or tokens of non-exclusivism.

Although much has been written about religious language (1.9), most of it concentrates on mythological or theological, rather than specifically performative, utterances.
Ritual language per se is seldom studied. Religious language
usually means God-language, ethical discourse, or mythic
narrative, any of which might occur in a rite but all three
of which are usually interpreted at a remove from ritual set-
tings. Typical is Grainger's The Language of the Rite,
which purports to be a general treatment of ritual language
but is, in fact, a Christianized theory of myth and defense
of ritual in general.

Since many scholars come to ritual studies with textually or verbally oriented training, an entree can sometimes be made through theories of "oral literature" that treat both narrative structure and performance. Both theological considerations of story and historical studies of ritual texts have so far neglected the insights of fieldstudy-oriented disciplines. Myth and ritual discussions need to consider myth as performance, not simply as text. Methodologically useful because of their attention to the act of telling stories are Jason's "A Multidimensional Approach to Oral Literature" and Georges' "Toward an Understanding of Storytelling Events" (see also Rayfield and Bauman).

Pieces like Ong's "African Talking Drums and Oral Noetics" and Ray's "'Performative Utterances' in African Rituals" (cf. Finnegan) are examples of writing that begins to bridge the chasm between linguistic and performative theory. The treatment of "ritual as language" (Lawson, Ferro-Luzzi) or "action as text" (Ricoeur) is useful, but seeing things metaphorically as language, grammar, or text can smother the overt quality of action if the metaphor is overextended, as I think it usually is. With the emergence of reception criticism, the acts of reading (see Stahl) and writing (see Lincoln; also see Ong, 1977b) are being seen, under certain conditions, as ritualized activities.

The study of sound, both musical and vocal, in ritual is still at a rudimentary stage. The "percussion and transition" debate between Needham, Jackson, and others made promising beginnings that have yet to be developed. Scholars in ritual studies need to establish a tentative link with musicology and the anthropology of dance (see, e.g., Royce) but are hesitant, probably because sound and movement are less amenable to linguistically inspired methods. The further consideration of mantras (Wheelock, 1980), curses, chants, and related forms of ritual utterance could lead in this direction.

2. RITUAL TYPES

Most English-language works on ritual are written either by theologians on Christian liturgy, anthropologists on the social functions of rites in preindustrial cultures, or historians

of religion on specific religious traditions in specified geographical areas. Among these three disciplines there is little consistency of terminological usage or consensus in identifying research priorities. Section two of the outline is far
from being a taxonomy. In fact, scrutinizing it illustrates
how profoundly scholarship in these fields has failed to produce one. There is little certainty in identifying either ritual's center or boundaries.

Certain ritual types, most notably worship (2.10),
are, with few exceptions, defined in Christian terms; others,
primarily magic (2.11), are construed to avoid the inclusion
of Christian manifestations. Certain terms, such as "festival" (2.4), "rite," and "ceremony" (2.7), are used technic-
ally and precisely by a few scholars and loosely, if not in-
terchangeably, by most others. "Rites of rebellion" (Gluckman) and "ritual inversion" (Babcock) overlap "liminality"
(Turner). A similar tangle exists if one tries to distinguish
"secular ritual" (Moore and Myerhoff), "civil ceremony" (Bellah), "interaction ritual" (Goffman), "public religion" (Wison;
Grimes, 1976), and "ritualization" (Huxley; Grimes, 1982).
The distinction between magic (2.11) and healing rites (2.12)
breaks down easily.

Certain terms, for instance, "purification" (2.6) and
"sacrifice" (2.9), are sometimes used to denote types, at
other times, phases within types. One of the types, meditation rites (2.14), is more often considered a subdivision
of mysticism than of ritual, with a resultant emphasis on
interiority rather than formalized exteriority. Some of the
types overlap, for instance, magic (2.11) and healing rites
(2.12), but bibliographers and scholars still use them as if
they were intelligible subdivisions.

Some lacunae in scholarly attention to ritual are obvious. I found very little on such universal ritual activities
as consecration, enshrinement, and procession. Histories
of rituals and ritual systems are rare despite the existence
of history of religions as a discipline. Likewise scarce are
studies of ritual's appropriation of ordinary actions such as
walking, sitting, eating, and breathing. Despite the wealth
of comparative materials on religion, little of it focuses
squarely on rites. When it does, it abstracts and compares
ritual motifs and consequently does not consider complete
ritual structures and processes or the shapes of whole ritual systems.

Rites of passage (2.1) denote a type that has been used by Van Gennep and others to include not only initiation and puberty rites but also marriages and funerals. I have split off the latter two for practical rather than theoretical reasons. At present any other type--in fact, any transitional phenomenon, e.g., becoming middle-aged--is subject to being considered "as" passage. Turner and the Turnerians, by appropriating Van Gennep's idea of liminality and extending it to include the "liminoid," have encompassed virtually every cultural transition and social drama, a procedure that sometimes threatens to distend the type.

The study of marriage ritual (2.2) is still largely dominated by anthropological analyses of kinship systems, so I find it more fruitful to read liturgical histories such as Stevenson's Nuptial Blessing: A Study of Christian Marriage Rites or something like the historical-sociological treatments of wedding processions and marriages in France found in Forster and Ranum's volume.

Some of the finest examples of studies of a ritual genre are on funerary rites (2.3), for instance, Huntington and Metcalf's Celebrations of Death. Their comparative case studies range from Borneo to Renaissance France and modern America; they maintain a balance between universalized and particularized considerations. Danforth's The Death Rituals of Rural Greece is more modest in scope but, because of its skillful use of photography, just as provocative.

On festivity (2.4) see Samuelson's excellent bibliography on Christmas. Also see Manning's collection The Celebration of Society and Turner's Celebrations, which was edited for the Smithsonian Institution's exhibition, "Celebration: A World of Art and Ritual"; the accompanying exhibition manual (Renwick) is finely annotated and elaborately illustrated. Not a great deal distinguishes festivity from inversion (2.15) --a matter of emphasis perhaps. Rites of inversion are discussed as if they more regularly lead to reflexivity, that is, cultural self-awareness (see Babcock).

Pilgrimages, processions, and parades (2.5) are grossly understudied although works on ritual space (1.2) often touch on them. Again, Turner's research (1978) largely determines the terrain.

Purification (2.6) and sacrifical rites (2.9) are often

studied in tandem. Douglas (1978) and Girard are stirring
the most controversy and interest. Hecht's recent bibliographical essay on sacrifice is a reliable guide to the recent
literature.

A body of materials on ceremony, or civil ritual (2.7),
continues to grow with Bellah as its fountainhead. A critique
of the view of ritual held in civil religion discussions is of-
fered by John Wilson. These discussions may eventually
overlap the Goffman-inspired consideration of interaction ritual (2.13), of which Heilman's Synagogue Life: A Study in
Symbolic Interaction is an interesting but cautious example.
In 1966 the study of face-to-face behavior converged with
the ethological study of ritualization among animals, but the
very important proceedings (see Huxley) of that gathering
have not yet been assimilated in the field of religious studies.

I suspect we will see a growing body of writing on ritual's role in ecology. Both Rappaport's Ecology, Meaning,
and Religion and Lincoln's Priests, Warriors, and Cattle: A
Study in the Ecology of Religions set ritual exchange (2.8)
in larger contexts than economics can handle.

The number of works on liturgy and worship (2.10)
is immense. I have included in the full bibliography only a
few that seem to have cross-cultural, comparative, or anthropological interest. "Rites of passage" and Christian "initiation" are terms that, for better or worse, seem to be gaining
popularity in liturgical circles. Both Smart and Parrinder
have written books that make worship a less in-house concept. Roy Rappaport is the only anthropologist to make serious use of the concept of liturgy; he has formulated a broad-
er, alternative view of it.

Most liturgical theologies continue to ignore anthropological and social scientific studies of ritual; those few writers who are beginning to admit such considerations still hold
them at the level of prolegomenon. Worgul's From Magic to
Metaphor is a good booklength instance; Hatchett, a shorter,
mechanically written one. Both make use of obvious theore-
ticians such as Van Gennep and Turner. Most of the essays
in Schmidt and Power's Liturgy and Cultural Religious Traditions are anthropologically serious in their treatment of indigenous religion. Hesser and Weigert have tried to formulate
a sociologically based set of variables for the comparative

study of liturgy. Among the most seminal liturgically minded
writings are those by Kavanagh, Scott, Schmemann, and Taft.

One book on the forefront of the liturgy-ritual discussion is Fenn's Liturgies and Trials, a superb volume that
compares the performative utterances of liturgies with those
of courtroom trials. Ware, like Fenn, utilizes the Austin-
Searle theory of performative utterance in interpreting liturgy but does so less successfully for academics, though
more usefully for pastors. Roberts' Initiation to Adulthood
employs Eliade, Van Gennep, and Turner and describes in
popular fashion a Protestant congregation's relatively suc-
cessful attempt to create and administer rites of passage to
its youth. The several volumes produced by the Sharing
Company (see Adams, for example) on sacred dance are useful Protestant how-to-do-it books that, by virtue of their
cross-cultural interests, transcend strictly in-house liturgics.
Browning, in "Festivity--From a Protestant Perspective,"
uses as much of Erikson, Pieper, and Martin as he thinks
one can utilize in Christian education circles.

Except for the essays by Kavanagh and Smith, The
Roots of Ritual (Shaughnessy)--a collection of papers from
what promised to be an important conference held by the
Murphy Center for Liturgical Research--is disappointing,
the contributions of Margaret Mead and Robert Bellah not-
withstanding.

Articles published in Worship and the Anglican Theological Review by Urban T. Holmes seem to me exemplary
writings by a theologian whose work is substantially, not
just superficially, open to symbolic anthropology. Sullivan
and Collins are also worth reading because of their attempt
to set Christian ritual symbolism in comparative-religious or
anthropological contexts.

Extraordinary attention is being focused on ritual healing (2.12) due partly to the emergence of medical anthropology and sociology, less to the impact of clinical and pastoral
psychology. Much of it, as one might imagine, is on hallucinogens, for example, Furst's Flesh of the Gods: The Ritual Use of Hallucinogens and Myerhoff's Peyote Hunt. One
difficulty with works on hallucinogens is that they can easily be diverted into the categories of ASC (altered states of
consciousness) research.

One of the most detrimental ritual and healing books,
The Way of the Shaman: A Guide to Power and Healing, is
a how-to-do-it volume by anthropologist Michael Harner.   By
ignoring cultural and religious contexts, it encourages the
worst tendencies of the ritual-starved.

I know of no theory that adequately differentiates and
relates magic (2.11), healing rites (2.12), and meditation
rites (2.14).   These types, like worship, are fraught with
we-they assumptions.   The book that comes nearest to sort-
ing out the mess is O'Keefe's brilliant volume on magic.   It
is destined, I believe, to become a classic because of its
comprehensiveness and lucidity in defining a type often made
useless by polemics and ethnocentrism.   The increasing
amount of attention being paid to rites of inversion (2.15)
and rebellion seems to imply a revision of our view of ritual
in general.   Babcock's collection of essays illustrates the
reversals embedded in even the most status-system oriented
rites.   A particularly worthwhile essay on inversion is McKim
Marriot's "The Feast of Love" (in Singer).

Since ritual sometimes includes or borders on drama,
I found it necessary to include "ritual drama" (2.16).   Ritual studies converge at significant points with performance
studies.   The journal entitled Performance Studies is evidence
of an expansion of the horizons of drama departments.   Performance studies include not only theater and ritual but also
sports and popular entertainments such as circus.   Consequently, it borders on popular culture (which also has a
journal in its own name).   Guttman's From Ritual to Record:
The Nature of Modern Sports and E. T. Kirby's Ur-Drama
are illustrations of the usefulness of interpreting ritual in
relation to its neighbors (play, sport, drama) rather than
its supposed opposites (mystical interiority, spontaneity, or
ordinary behavior).   Grotowski's ritualized "paratheatrical"
experiments lie behind this expanded view of performance;
his pithy but enigmatic works on "poor" and "holy" theater
are essential reading in ritual studies.   A useful and visual-
ly provocative book is Coult's documentation of Welfare State
International of England, one of the most ingenious groups
of post-modern celebration makers.

3.   RITUAL DESCRIPTIONS

Since rituals classify and construct cosmologies, classi-

fying rituals themselves is difficult; one easily lapses into
meta-ritual while doing it.   In many instances of classifying
works for this bibliography I simply relied on a key word in
a title. For example, in the following article the obvious
word is "sacrifice." However, a careful reading of Benjamin
Beit-Hallahmi's "Sacrifice, Fire, and the Victory of the Sun:
A Search for the Origins of Hanukkah" (cf. Deshen) reveals
that it could be classed under festivals, sacrifice, purification rites, rites of rebellion (inasmuch as Hanukkah recol-
lects the story of the rebellion against the Syrians), or ritual space (because it commemorates the rededication of the
Temple). Many books and articles on ritual use multiple
analytical categories and classificatory types. Others cir-
cumvent them, and still others stick closely to the indigenous terminology of ritualists themselves. So the key-word
tactic, which is problematic even when it can be applied,
breaks down; hence the necessity for a third section in my
categorization, Ritual Descriptions.

        As I use the term, it is broader than "ritual accounts."
A ritual account is a self-conscious attempt to produce documentation relatively free of overt interpretive intrusion or
theoretical analysis; a ritual description does not exclude
theoretical and typological considerations on principle but
simply keeps them in low profile. One could include both
ritual texts (produced by ritualists) and ritual accounts
(produced by observers) as variants of ritual description;
I have not attempted to gather the former.

        The category "Ritual Descriptions" includes works
whose titles do not refer to either a commonly employed ritual category or a type. Their primary frame of reference,
on the surface at least, is the tradition, system, period, or
geographical area from which a rite comes. An example is
Robert Bocock's Ritual in Industrial Society, a sociological
approach to English rituals, including coronations, Anglican
worship, life-cycle observances, and esthetic performances.
Another is Scullard's Festivals and Ceremonies of the Roman
Republic, a month-by-month historical study of the Roman
calendar and its ritual cycle. In many such works historical
or descriptive concerns have a higher profile than theoretical ones do. For this reason, most of the entries one would
associate with history (4.6) are in this third section.

        Much writing about ritual is contained in books on the
religions and cultures in which they are embedded, e.g.,

Wolf's Religion and Ritual in Chinese Society. This is es-
pecially true of anthropological studies such as Ortiz's The
Tewa World or Geertz's The Religion of Java. For purposes
of comparative or cross-cultural ritual study this is as it
should be, provided the ritual materials per se can be identified. A carefully introduced and annotated anthology of
such materials is needed; the much used Reader in Comparative Religion (Lessa and Vogt) is too broadly focused and
too exclusively anthropological to fill this need.

The materials in section three sometimes include por-
tions of ritual texts and exegesis, along with ritual accounts,
summaries, and interpretations. Sometimes the accounts are
narrative in style ("This happened, then that"), then some
of them leap to theoretical generalizations about the intention
or function of a ritual. If there are middle steps, they often consist of a discussion of the rite's symbols (treating
them as "building blocks") or a record of participants' comments (see, e.g., Turner's Chihamba the White Spirit: A
Ritual Drama of the Ndembu). Full accounts of rituals are
usually tedious, often long, and therefore rarely published.
Without commentary they are less intelligible than myths;
with it they are ponderous. And a mere summary of a ritual intention, type, or function either fails to convince or
has to be accepted on the author's word. So the question
of style in reporting and interpreting rituals is a serious
one. Between liturgical commentary and ethnographic documentation is a great chasm, which will necessitate considerable
attention to style in ritual studies. A good example of a
work that combines both humanistic and analytical elements
in its style is Myerhoff's Number Our Days, a study of life
in a center for elderly Jewish people. Among questions the
field must come to terms with are how much to describe,
what to summarize, how prominent to make the authorial
voice, and how to move from tightly focused exegesis to
generalization (or vice-versa).

4. GENERAL WORKS

In the final portion of the bibliography I have gathered
works not listed in earlier sections but helpful in formulating
a coherent theoretical basis for understanding ritual. The
number of general theoretical volumes is large if one lists
those with important but largely unrecognized implications

for the study of ritual. Few scholars in religious studies would think of looking for Angeloglou's A History of Make-Up, and not too many would deliberately set out to find Royce's Anthropology of Dance or Siirala's The Voice of Illness. But these books make significant contributions to understanding how people stylize and objectify the human body, a central consideration of ritual studies.

What is true of titles is also true of certain fields. Most scholars writing on ritual think to look to anthropology or liturgics, perhaps to theater, but seldom to literature, education, or biology. They would overlook two writers-- one in kinesics (4.7), the other in biogenetics (4.8)--who are on the forefront of the study of gesture. Ray Birdwhistell's Kinesics in Context and Eugene d'Aquili's The Spectrum of Ritual: A Biogenetic Structural Analysis are opening up ways that can lead to the interpretation of ritual at the gestural (in contrast to, say, typological or functional) level. And in education (4.9) a number of theorists (Burnett, Kapferer, and Olson) have begun to identify "rituals of the hidden curriculum" (Gherke) and link drama in the classroom to ritualized ways of knowing (Courtney). Many of the educationalists are depending on Erikson's seminal essay, "The Development of Ritualization."

Materials in theater, drama criticism, and performance theory are mushrooming. In addition to Schechner's works, David Cole's The Theatrical Event: A Mythos, a Vocabulary, a Perspective is the most sensitive to theater's connection with shamanism.

General works in the anthropology (4.2) of religion or symbolism, such as the collections of essays edited by Brian Wilson, Carole Hill, and Robert Spenser, far outnumber significant studies by sociologists (4.3). I have already referred to some of the most important anthropological works. As for sociology, Nagendra has tried to summarize some of the ways ritual is conceived among its modern theorists, and Goody has posed some severe criticisms of the utility of ritual as a theoretical category for use in the social sciences. The journal Zygon (18/3 [1983]) has recently devoted an entire issue to the theme "Ritual in Human Adaptation," a fine illustration of convergence and conflicts in the scientific and humanistic study of ritual.

Burke and Frye remain the dominant literary (4.4) theorists of ritual, but Girard is rapidly displacing them. They, along with Eliade, Jung, Van Gennep, and Freud, typically lie behind treatments of ritual in literature, for instance, Vargo's Rainstorms and Fire: Ritual in the Novels of John Updike and Rupp's Celebration in Postwar American Fiction or the two older collections of short stories plus essays, The Rite of Becoming: Stories and Studies of Adolescence (Waldhorn) and The Scapegoat: Ritual and Literature (Vickery). In my estimation a promising direction in the study of ritual and literature is Barbara Babcock-Abrahams' suggestive "The Novel and the Carnival World." Though she considers only the "carnivalized" novel, the obvious choice for those inspired by symbolic-anthropological theories of the liminoid, her tentatively posed methods are applicable to other genres.

Religion and literature as a discipline needs to attend to its counterpart, anthropology and literature (see, e.g., Myerhoff and Metzger). Someone also needs to bridge the gap in theory that separates a book like Fiction and Repetition (Miller) from one like Kierkegaard's Repetition and both, in turn, from psychoanalytic theories of repetition and Eliade's idea of eternal return. Altizer has already leaped into the fray with his Hegel-inspired claim, "Literature is ritual which has passed into its own inherent 'other'" (275). Until the field of ritual studies formulates a theory of repetition centered in ritual performance and open toward literary and psychological concepts, it will be condemned to summarizing and parasitic borrowing. Other works that are useful in studying ritual's relation to literature are those by Cabaniss, Brophy, Simms, and Stein--all applied works. The most comprehensive review of this area is Hardin's "Ritual in Recent Criticism."

In religious studies (4.1), which are not always distinct from theology and liturgics, ritual seems to be a growing concern both as a theme in works not explicitly on ritual and as a metaphor for interpreting other cultural phenomena. To illustrate the first, in Tom Driver's Patterns of Grace it lies just below the surface, but in 1981 he began making overt use of his field studies of ritual in Haiti to interpret the eucharist (167 ff.). And to illustrate the second, Gregor Goethals' The TV Ritual: Worship at the Video Altar makes ritualizing the key metaphor in her analysis of popular visual icons.

As philosophers of religion and theologians push at the limits of religious language and belief, metaphors that once identified the sacred with height, depth, or inwardness seem to be giving way to ones that allow for a positive evaluation of surfaces, exteriority, and overt action. For example, Comstock's "A Behavioral Approach to the Sacred" and Kliever's "Fictive Religion: Rhetoric and Play," as well as his "Story and Space," are not about ritual as such but seem to imply it as a next obvious step. Doty's comprehensive definition of myth takes that step and makes explicit connection with a theory of ritual (see also Pilgrim).

Two persistent issues in these discussions are (a) When theorizing about ritual, how should we conceive the relation between feeling and form? and (b) What constitutes the "truth" of ritual and play (see Hardwick)? Even though the theology of play (Neale) has withered in religious studies, anthropology and performance studies (see Turner 1982b; Schechner and Schuman) continue to elaborate and sharpen play theory in a way that compels ritual studies to attend to it.

Eliade is losing his position as primary theorist of symbol, myth, and ritual. But despite sustained critiques of him (see Dudley), no theoretical alternative of similar stature has arisen within the field. Nevertheless, there are piecemeal theoretical beginnings that promise alternatives. I have both posed and criticized some of them in Beginnings in Ritual Studies (1982); (see also Grimes, forthcoming). One of the most provocative alternatives is the work of Jonathan Z. Smith, a historian of religion. Chapters 3, 4, and 6 of Imagining Religion and chapters 4, 5, 6, and 13 of Map Is Not Territory are absolutely essential for both their critique of Eliade's understanding of sacred space and their vigorous advocacy of a methodology and taxonomy that refuse to accord religion, and thereby ritual, a privileged status. His criticism of symbol-hunting, insistence on the ordinariness of religion, and attention to incongruity and lack of systematic integration are well argued (see 1982, 18,63).

No one has yet carefully compared his definition of ritual as "a means of performing the way things ought to be in conscious tension to the way things are in such a way that this ritualized perfection is recollected in the ordinary, uncontrolled, course of things" (Smith, 1982, 63) with the ones formulated by Delattre and implied by Jennings. I share

with Smith a suspicion that definitions easily become mono-
thetic, but, if pressed, definitions can germinate useful
theories. Use and further reflection are the only ways to
draw out definitions so their implications can be refined.

John Dixon is a theologian-art historian. I cannot
imagine two theorists more methodologically opposed than he
and Smith, yet both are concerned with theories of sacred
space. Although Dixon has yet to write explicitly on ritual,
his attention to embodiment, form, and space is consistent
and sustained. His theory of "the dramatics of the self" in
The Physiology of Faith (part 3) leads clearly and reliably
to basic issues in ritual studies.

Jennings' "On Ritual Knowledge" and Zuesse's "Meditation on Ritual," like Dixon's "The Erotics of Knowing," in-
sist on the epistemological primacy of the body, as well as
the exploratory (not just confirmatory) possibilities of ritual
action. Delattre's "Ritual Resourcefulness and Cultural
Pluralism," by defining ritual as a means of articulating "the
felt shape and rhythm of our own humanity" (1978, 282),
would seem to be in fundamental agreement with one of Dixon's maxims, "Symbol gives rhythm its structure, rhythm
gives symbol its energy" (1979, 91). The field of ritual
studies will have earned its keep if it can press pithy aph-
orisms like this one into yielding more precise vocabulary
and more comprehensive theory.

REFERENCES

Adams, Doug. 1977. Congregational Dancing in Christian
    Worship. Austin, TX: Sharing.

Altizer, Thomas J. J. 1980. "Ritual and Contemporary
    Repetition." Dialog 19:274-280.

Angeloglou, Maggie. 1970. A History of Make-Up. New
    York: Macmillan.

Babcock, Barbara A., ed. 1978. The Reversible World:
    Symbolic Inversion in Art and Society. Ithaca, NY:
    Cornell University Press.

Babcock-Abrahams, Barbara. 1974. "The Novel and the

Carnival World." Modern Language Notes: Comparative
Literature 89/6:911-937.

Beit-Hallahmi, B. 1976-77. "Sacrifice, Fire, and the Victory of the Sun: A Search for the Origins of Hanukkah."
Psychoanalytic Review 63/4:497-509.

Bocock, Robert. 1974. Ritual in Industrial Society: A Sociological Analysis of Ritualism in Modern England. London: Allen & Unwin.

Bauman, Richard. 1975. "Verbal Art as Performance."
American Anthropologist 77/2:290-311.

Bellah, Robert N. 1975. The Broken Covenant: American
Civil Religion in Time of Trial. New York: Seabury.

Birdwhistell, Ray L. 1970. Kinesics and Context: Essays
on Body Motion Communication. Philadelphia: University
of Pennsylvania Press.

Brophy, Robert J. 1973. Robinson Jeffers: Myth, Ritual
and Symbol in His Narrative Poems. Cleveland: Case-
Western.

Browning, Robert. 1980. "Festivity--From a Protestant
Perspective." Religious Education 75/3:273-281.

Burke, Kenneth. 1966. Language as Symbolic Action.
Berkeley: University of California Press.

_____. 1969. A Grammar of Motives. Berkeley: Uni-
versity of California Press.

_____. 1970. The Rhetoric of Religion. Berkeley: Uni-
versity of California Press.

Burnett, Jaquetta Hill. 1969. "Ceremony, Rites, and Economy in the Student System of an American High School."
Human Organization 28:1-10.

Cabaniss, Allen. 1970. Liturgy and Literature. University,
AL: University of Alabama Press.

Cole, David. 1975. The Theatrical Event: A Mythos, a

Vocabulary, a Perspective. Middletown, CT: Wesleyan
University.

Collins, Mary. 1975. "Liturgical Methodology and the Cultural Evolution of Worship in the United States." Worship
49/2:85-102.

_____. 1979. "Critical Ritual Studies: Examining an In-
tersection of Theology and Culture" in The Bent World:
Essays on Religion and Culture. Ed. John A. May. Chico,
CA: Scholars Press.

Comstock, W. Richard. 1981. "A Behavioral Approach to
the Sacred: Category Formation in Religious Studies."
Journal of the American Academy of Religion 49/4:625-643.

Coult, Tony, and Baz Kershaw, eds. 1983. Engineers of
the Imagination: The Welfare State Handbook. London:
Methuen.

Courtney, Richard. 1974. Play, Drama, and Thought: The
Intellectual Background to Drama in Education. 2nd rev.
ed. New York: Drama Books.

_____. 1970. The Dramatic Curriculum. London, Ont.:
University of Western Ontario Press.

Danforth, Loring M. 1982. The Death Rituals of Rural
Greece. Photos by Alexander Tsiaras. Princeton, NJ:
Princeton University Press.

d'Aquili, Eugene D., et al. 1979. The Spectrum of Ritual:
A Biogenetic Structural Analysis. New York: Columbia
University Press.

Delattre, Roland. 1978. "Ritual Resourcefulness and Cultural Pluralism." Soundings 61/3:281-301.

Deshen, Shlomo. 1979. "The Kol Nidre Enigma: An Anthropological View of the Day of Atonement Liturgy." Ethnology 18/2:121-133.

Doty, William. 1980. "Mythophiles' Dyscrasia: A Comprehensive Definition of Myth." Journal of the American
Academy of Religion 48/4:531-602.

Douglas, Mary. 1973. Natural Symbols: Explorations in Cosmology. New York: Random House.

_____. 1978. Purity and Danger: An Analysis of Concepts of Pollution and Taboo. Boston: Routledge.

Dixon, John, Jr. 1973. "The Metaphoric Transformation, An Essay on the Physiology of the Imagination." Sociological Analysis 34/1:56-74.

_____. 1974. "The Erotics of Knowing." Anglican Theological Review 56/1:3-16.

_____. 1977. "Theology and Form: Reflections on the Spaces of the Imagination." Journal of the American Academy of Religion 45/2 (Supplement):593-622.

_____. 1979. The Physiology of Faith: A Theory of Theological Relativity. New York: Harper & Row.

Driver, Tom F. 1977. Patterns of Grace: Human Experience as Word of God. New York: Harper & Row.

_____. 1981. Christ in a Changing World: Toward an Ethical Christology. New York: Crossroad.

Dudley, Guilford, III. 1977. Religion on Trial: Mircea Eliade and His Critics. Philadelphia: Temple University Press.

Durkheim, Emile. 1965. The Elementary Forms of Religious Life. Trans. Joseph W. Swain. New York: Free Press.

Eliade, Mircea. 1954. The Myth of the Eternal Return. New York: Pantheon.

_____. 1958. Patterns in Comparative Religion. New York: Sheed.

_____. 1958. Yoga, Immortality and Freedom. Princeton, NJ: Princeton University Press.

_____. 1959. The Sacred and the Profane. New York: Harcourt.

_____. 1959. Cosmos and History. New York: Harper
& Row.

_____. 1961. Images and Symbols. New York: Sheed.

_____. 1962. The Forge and the Crucible. New York:
Harper & Row.

_____. 1964. Shamanism: Archaic Techniques of Ecstasy.
Princeton, NJ: Princeton University Press.

_____. 1965. Rites and Symbols of Initiation. New York:
Harper & Row.

Erikson, Erik. 1968. "The Development of Ritualization" in
The Religious Situation 1968. Boston: Beacon.

_____. 1977. Toys and Reasons: Stages in the Rituali-
zation of Life. New York: Norton.

Feldstein, Leonard. 1976. "The Human Body as Rhythm
and Symbol: A Study in Practical Hermeneutics." The
Journal of Medicine and Philosophy 1/2:136-161.

Fenn, Richard K. 1982. Liturgies and Trials: The Secularization of Religious Language. New York: Pilgrim.

Fernandez, James. 1974. "The Mission of Metaphor in Expressive Culture." Current Anthropology 15:119-145.

Ferro-Luzzi, Gabriella Eithinger. 1977. "Ritual as Language:
The Case of South Indian Food Offerings." Current Anthropology 18/3:507-514.

Finnegan, Ruth. 1969. "How to Do Things with Words:
Performative Utterances Among the Limba of Sierra
Leone." MAN (N.S.) 4:537-552.

Firth, Raymond. 1973. Symbols: Public and Private.
Ithaca, NY: Cornell University Press.

Forster, Robert, and Orest Ranum, eds. 1982. Ritual,
Religion, and the Sacred. Baltimore: Johns Hopkins
University Press.

Freud, Sigmund. The Standard Edition of the Complete Psychological Works of Sigmund Freud (SE). Ed. & trans. James Strachey. London: Hogarth.

_____. 1953. "Totem and Taboo." SE 13:1-161.

_____. 1959. "Obsessive Actions and Religious Practices." SE 9:116-127.

_____. 1961. "The Future of An Illusion." SE 21:3-56.

_____. 1964. "Moses and Monotheism." SE 1964:3-137.

Frye, Northrop. 1968. Anatomy of Criticism. New York: Atheneum.

Furst, Peter T., ed. 1972. Flesh of the Gods. The Ritual Use of Hallucinogens. New York: Praeger.

Gay, Volney. 1979. Freud on Ritual: Reconstruction and Critique. Missoula, MT: Scholars Press.

Geertz, Clifford. 1960. The Religion of Java. Glencoe, IL: Free Press.

_____. 1966. "Religion as a Cultural System" in Anthropological Approaches to the Study of Religion. Ed. Michael Brown. London: Tavistock.

Gehrke, Nathalie. 1979. "Rituals of the Hidden Curriculum" in Children's Time and Space. Ed. Kaoru Yamamoto. New York: Teachers College.

Georges, Robert. 1969. "Toward an Understanding of Storytelling Events." Journal of American Folklore 82: 313-328.

Gill, Sam. 1975. "Color in Navajo Ritual Symbolism: An Evaluation of Methods." Journal of Anthropological Research 31:350-363.

Girard, Rene. 1977. Violence and the Sacred. Trans. Patrick Gregory. Baltimore: Johns Hopkins University Press.

Gluckman, Max. 1954. Rituals of Rebellion in Southeast Africa. Manchester, Eng.: Manchester University Press.

Goffman, Erving. 1967. Interaction Ritual: Essays on Face-to-Face Behavior. Garden City, NY: Doubleday.

Goethals, Gregor T. 1981. The TV Ritual: Worship at the Video Altar. Boston: Beacon.

Goody, Jack. 1961. "Religion and Ritual: The Definitional Problems." British Journal of Sociology 12/2:142-164.

Grainger, Roger. 1974. The Language of the Rite. London: Darton.

Grimes, Ronald L. 1976. Symbol and Conquest: Public Ritual of Drama in Santa Fe, New Mexico. Ithaca, NY: Cornell.

_____. 1982. Beginnings in Ritual Studies. Washington, DC: University Press.

_____. Forthcoming. "Ritual Studies." The Encyclopaedia of Religion. Ed. Mircea Eliade. New York: Macmillan and Free Press.

Grotowski, Jerzy. 1973. "Holiday: The Day That Is Holy." The Drama Review 17/2:113-119.

Guttman, Allen. 1978. From Ritual to Record: The Nature of Modern Sports. New York: Columbia University Press.

Hardin, Richard. 1983. "'Ritual' in Recent Criticism: The Elusive Sense of Community." PMLA 98/5:846-862.

Harner, Michael. 1980. The Way of the Shaman: A Guide to Power and Healing. New York: Harper & Row.

Hardwick, Charley D. 1981. "Elusive Religiosity, Illusions, and Truth Telling." Journal of the American Academy of Religion 49/4:645-655.

Hatchett, Marion. 1976. Sanctifying Life, Time, and Space: An Introduction to Liturgical Study. New York: Seabury.

A Programmatic Essay   25

Hecht, Richard. 1982. "Studies on Sacrifice." Religious
Studies Review 8/3:253-259.

Heilman, Samuel C. 1976. Synagogue Life: A Study in
Symbolic Interaction. Chicago: University of Chicago
Press.

Hesser, Garry, and Andrew Weigert. 1980. "Comparative
Dimensions of Liturgy: A Conceptual Framework and
Feasibility Application." Sociological Analysis 41/3:215-
229.

Hill, Carole, ed. 1975. Symbols and Society: Essays on
Belief Systems in Action. Athens, GA: Southern Anthropological Society.

Holmes, Urban T. 1973. "Liminality and Liturgy." Worship
47/7:386-399.

_____. 1974. "What has Manchester to do with Jerusalem."
Anglican Theological Review 59/1:79-97.

_____. 1977. "Ritual and the Social Drama." Worship
51:197-213.

Huntington, Richard, and Peter Metcalf. 1979. Celebrations
of Death: The Anthropology of Mortuary Ritual. Cambridge, Eng.: Cambridge University Press.

Huxley, Sir Julian. 1966. "A Discussion on Ritualization of
Behavior in Animals and Man." Philosophical Transactions
of the Royal Society of London. Series B, 251:247-526.

Jackson, Anthony. 1968. "Sound and Ritual." MAN (NS)
3/2:293-299.

Jarvie, I. C. 1976. "On the Limits of Symbolic Interpretation in Anthropology." Current Anthropology 17:687-701.

Jason, Heda. 1969. "A Multidimensional Approach to Oral
Literature." Current Anthropology 10:413-426.

Jennings, Theodore W. 1982. "On Ritual Knowledge." The
Journal of Religion 62/2:111-127.

Jung, C. G. The Collected Works of C. G. Jung (CW).
    Trans. R. F. C. Hull. Princeton, NJ: Princeton Uni-
    versity Press.

_____. 1963. "Mysterium Coniunctionis." CW 14.

_____. 1963. "Psychology of Religion." CW 11.

_____. 1967. "Symbols of Transformation." 2nd ed.
    CW 5.

_____. 1968. "The Archetypes and the Collective Un-
    conscious." 2nd ed. CW 9/1.

_____. 1968(b). "Aion: Researches into the Phenomen-
    ology of the Self." CW 9/2.

_____. 1968(c). "Alchemical Studies." CW 13.

_____. 1968(d). "Psychology and Alchemy." CW 12.

Kapferer, Judith. 1981. "Socialization and the Symbolic
    Order." Anthropology and Education Quarterly 12/4:258-
    274.

Kavanagh, Aidan. 1982. Elements of Ritual: A Handbook
    of Liturgical Style. New York: Pueblo.

Kierkegaard, Søren. 1946. Repetition: An Essay in Ex-
    perimental Psychology. Trans. Walter Lowrie. Princeton,
    NJ: Princeton University Press.

Kippenberg, H. G., ed. 1982. Visible Religion: Annual
    for Religious Iconography. Leiden: Brill.

Kirby, E. T. 1975. Ur-Drama: The Origins of Theatre.
    New York: Dutton.

Kliever, Lonnie. 1977. "Story and Space: The Forgotten
    Dimension." Journal of the American Academy of Religion,
    Supplement 45/2:529-563.

_____. 1979. "Polysymbolism and Modern Religiosity."
    Journal of Religion 59:169-194.

_____. 1981. "Fictive Religion: Rhetoric and Play."
Journal of the American Academy of Religion 49/4:658-669.

Lawson, E. Thomas. 1976. "Ritual as Language." Religion
6:123-139.

Lessa, William, and Evon Vogt, eds. 1965. Reader in Comparative Religion: An Anthropological Approach. 3rd ed.
New York: Harper & Row.

Lincoln, Bruce. 1977. "Two Notes on Modern Rituals."
Journal of the American Academy of Religion 45/2:147-160.

_____. 1981. Priests, Warriors and Cattle: A Study in
the Ecology of Religions. Berkeley: University of California Press.

Lodrick, Deryek O. 1981. Sacred Cows, Sacred Places:
Origins and Survivals of Animal Homes in India. Berkeley: University of California Press.

Manning, Frank, ed. 1983. The Celebration of Society:
Perspectives on Cultural Performance. London, Canada:
Congress of Social and Humanistic Studies.

Martin, Gerhard M. 1976. Fest: The Transformation of
the Everyday. Philadelphia: Fortress.

Mead, George Herbert. 1934. Mind, Self, and Society.
Chicago: University of Chicago Press.

_____. 1938. The Philosophy of the Act. Chicago:
University of Chicago Press.

Miller, J. Hillis. 1982. Fiction and Repetition: Seven
English Novels. Cambridge, MA: Harvard University
Press.

Moore, Sally Falk, and Barbara Myerhoff. 1977. Secular
Ritual. Assen, The Netherlands: Van Gorcum.

Myerhoff, Barbara. 1974. Peyote Hunt: The Sacred Journey of the Huichol Indians. Ithaca, NY: Cornell.

_____. 1978. Number Our Days. New York: Simon and
Schuster.

_____, and Deena Metzger. 1980. "The Journal As Ac-
tivity and Genre: Or Listening to the Silent Laughter of
Mozart." Semiotica 30/1-2:97-114.

Nagendra, S. P. 1971. The Concept of Ritual in Modern
Sociological Theory. New Delhi: Academic Journals of
India.

Neale, Robert E. 1969. In Praise of Play: Toward a Psychology of Religion. New York: Harper & Row.

Needham, Rodney. 1967. "Percussion and Transition."
Man (N.S.) 2:606-614.

O'Keefe, Daniel L. 1982. Stolen Lightning: The Social
Theory of Magic. New York: Continuum.

Olson, Wayne. 1979. "Ceremony as Religious Education."
Religious Education 74/6:563-569.

Ong, Walter J. 1977(a). "African Drums and Oral Noetics."
New Literary History 8/3:411-429.

_____. 1977(b). "Maranatha: Death and Life in the
Text of the Book." Journal of the American Academy of
Religion 45/4:419-449.

Ortiz, Alfonso. 1969. The Tewa World: Space, Time, Being
and Becoming in a Pueblo Society. Chicago: University of
Chicago Press.

Paige, Karen Erikson, and Jeffrey M. Paige. 1981. The
Politics of Reproductive Ritual. Berkeley: University of
California Press.

Parrinder, Geoffrey. 1976. Worship in the World's Religions.
Totowa, NJ: Littlefield.

Pieper, Josef. 1965. In Tune with the World. New York:
Harcourt.

Pilgrim, Richard B. 1978. "Ritual" in Introduction to the
Study of Religion. Ed. T. William Hall. New York:
Harper & Row.

Quasten, Johannes. 1983. Music and Worship in Pagan and
   Christian Antiquity. Trans. Boniface Ramsey. Washington, DC: National Association of Pastoral Musicians.

Rappaport, Roy A. 1979. Ecology, Meaning, and Religion.
   Richmond, CA: North Atlantic Books.

Ray, Benjamin. 1973. "'Performative Utterances' in African
   Rituals." History of Religions 13/1:16-35.

Rayfield, J. R. 1972. "What Is a Story?" American Anthropologist 74:1085-1106.

Renwick Gallery. 1982. Celebration: A World of Art and
   Ritual. Washington, DC: Smithsonian Institution.

Ricoeur, Paul. 1973. "The Model of the Text: Meaningful
   Action Considerations as a Text." New Literary History
   5/1:91-117.

Roberts, William O., Jr. 1982. Initiation to Adulthood: An
   Ancient Rite of Passage in Contemporary Form. New York:
   Pilgrim.

Royce, Anya Peterson. 1980. The Anthropology of Dance.
   Bloomington: Indiana University Press.

Rupp, Richard. 1970. Celebration in Postwar American Fiction. Coral Gables, FL: University of Miami Press.

Samuelson, Sue. 1982. Christmas: An Annotated Bibliography of Analytical Scholarship. New York: Garland.

Saunders, E. Dale. 1960. Mudra: A Study of Symbolic
   Gestures in Japanese Buddhist Sculpture. Princeton, NJ:
   Princeton University Press.

Schechner, Richard. 1977. Essays on Performance Theory,
   1970-1976. New York: Drama Books.

_____. 1981. "Restoration of Behavior." Studies in the
   Anthropology of Visual Communication 8:2-45.

_____, and Mady Schuman, eds. 1976. Ritual, Play, and

Performance: Readings in the Social Sciences/Theatre.
New York: Seabury.

Schmemann, Alexander. 1963. "Theology and Liturgical
Tradition" in Worship in Scripture and Tradition. Ed.
Massey Shepherd. Oxford, Eng.: Oxford University
Press.

Schmidt, Herman, and David Power, eds. 1977. Liturgy
and Cultural Religious Traditions. New York: Seabury.

Scott, R. Taylor. 1980. "The Likelihood of Liturgy."
Anglican Theological Review 62:103-120.

Scullard, H. H. 1981. Festivals and Ceremonies of the
Roman Republic. Ithaca, NY: Cornell University Press.

Searle, John. 1969. Speech Acts. Cambridge, Eng.: Cambridge University Press.

Shaughnessy, James D., ed. 1973. The Roots of Ritual.
Grand Rapids, MI: Eerdmans.

Simms, Norman. 1975. Ritual and Rhetoric: Intellectual
and Ceremonial Backgrounds to Middle English Literature.
Folcroft, PA: Folcroft.

Siirala, Aarne. 1981. The Voice of Illness: A Study in
Therapy and Prophecy. 2nd ed. New York: Mellen.

Singer, Milton, ed. 1966. Krishna: Myths, Rites and
Attitudes. Chicago: University of Chicago Press.

Smart, Ninian. 1972. The Concept of Worship. New York:
St. Martin.

Smith, Jonathan Z. 1978. Map Is Not Territory: Studies
in the History of Religion. Leiden: Brill.

_____. 1982. Imagining Religion: From Babylon to
Jonestown. Chicago: University of Chicago Press.

Smith-Rosenberg, Carroll. 1975. "The Female World of
Love and Ritual: Relations Between Women in Nineteenth
Century America." Signs: Journal of Women in Culture
and Society 1/1:1-29.

Solberg, Winton. 1977. Redeem the Time: The Puritan
Sabbath in Early America. Cambridge, MA: Harvard
University Press.

Spencer, Robert, ed. 1969. Forms of Symbolic Action.
Seattle: University of Washington.

Sperber, Dan. 1975. Rethinking Symbolism. Trans. Alice
L. Merton. Cambridge, Eng.: Cambridge University
Press.

Staal, Frits. 1979. "The Meaninglessness of Ritual."
Numen 26:2-22.

Stahl, Abraham. 1979. "Ritualistic Reading Among Jews."
Anthropological Quarterly 52/2:115-120.

Stein, Richard L. 1975. The Ritual of Interpretation: The
Fine Arts as Literature in Ruskin, Rossetti and Pater.
Cambridge, MA: Harvard University Press.

Stevenson, Kenneth. 1983. Nuptial Blessing: A Study of
Christian Marriage Rites. Oxford, Eng.: Oxford University Press.

Sullivan, H. Patrick. 1975. "Ritual: Attending to the
World." Anglican Theological Review, Supplementary
Series No. 5:9-32.

Taft, Robert. 1978. "The Structural Analysis of Liturgical
Units: An Essay in Methodology." Worship 52:315-329.

Thompson, Robert F. 1974. African Art in Motion: Icon
and Act. Berkeley: University of California Press.

Turner, Victor W. 1962. Chihamlia the White Spirit: A
Ritual Drama of the Ndembu. Manchester, Eng.: Manchester University Press.

_____. 1967. The Forest of Symbols. Ithaca, NY:
Cornell University Press.

_____. 1968. "Myth and Symbol" in International Ency-
clopaedia of Social Sciences. Ed. David Sills. London:
Macmillan.

_____. 1969. The Ritual Process. Chicago: Aldine.

_____. 1974. Dramas, Fields and Metaphors. Ithaca,
NY: Cornell University Press.

_____. 1978. Images and Pilgrimage in Christian Culture.
New York: Columbia.

_____. 1982(a). Celebration: Studies in Festivity and
Ritual. Washington, DC: Smithsonian Institution.

_____. 1982(b). Fron Ritual to Theatre: The Human
Seriousness of Play. New York: Performing Arts.

Van Gennep, Arnold. 1960. The Rites of Passage. Chicago:
University of Chicago Press.

Vargo, Edward. 1973. Rainstorms and Fire: Ritual in the
Novels of John Updike. Port Washington, NY: Kennikat.

Vickery, John B., and J'nan M. Sellery, eds. 1972. The
Scapegoat: Ritual and Literature. Boston: Houghton
Mifflin.

Waldhorn, Arthur and Hilda, eds. 1966. The Rite of Becoming: Stories and Studies of Adolescence. New York:
New American Library.

Ware, James H., Jr. 1981. Not with Words of Wisdom:
Performative Language and Liturgy. Washington, DC:
University Press of America.

Warner, Maria. 1978. Alone of All Her Sex: The Myth and
Cult of the Virgin Mary. New York: Knopf.

Wheelock, Wade. 1980. "A Taxonomy of the Mantras in the
New- and Full-Moon Sacrifice." History of Religions
19/4:349-369.

_____. 1982. "The Problem of Ritual Language: From
Information to Situation." Journal of the American Academy of Religion 50/1:49-71.

Wigley, John. 1980. The Rise and Fall of the Victorian
Sunday. Manchester, Eng.: University of Manchester.

Wilson, Brian, ed. 1970. Rationality. New York: Harper
& Row.

Wilson, John F. 1979. Public Religion in American Culture.
Philadelphia: Temple University Press.

Wolf, Arthur P., ed. 1974. Religion and Ritual in Chinese
Society. Stanford, CA: Stanford University Press.

Worgul, George S. 1980. From Magic to Metaphor: A Validation of the Christian Sacraments. New York: Paulist.

RESEARCH IN RITUAL STUDIES:

THE BIBLIOGRAPHY

PART 1. RITUAL COMPONENTS

1.1 ACTION
(Movement, Dance, Performance, Mime, Music,
Rhythm, Gesture, Play, Work)

1 Adams, Doug. 1971. Congregational Dancing in Christian Worship. Rev. ed. 1977. Austin, TX: Sharing Co.

2 Alenikoff, F. 1973. "Performance: The Whirling Dervishes of Turkey." Craft Horizons 33:13.

3 Armstrong, L. 1977. "Shepherd's Dance in the Basque Country --December 1976." Folklore 88:211-14.

4 Bandem, I. M. 1975. "Baris Dance." Ethnomusicology 19: 259-65.

5 Bayer, Raymond. 1953. "The Essence of Rhythm," in Reflections on Art. Ed. Suzanne K. Langer. New York: Oxford University Press.

6 Brenneman, Walter L., Jr., et al. 1982. "The Body of Ritual: Gesture, Movement, and Motion." Ch. 6 of their The Seeing Eye: Hermeneutical Phenomenology in the Study of Religion. University Park, PA: Pennsylvania State University Press.

7 Britton, K. 1979. "Symbolic Actions and Objects: The Weak Pipe and the Little Drum." Philosophy 54:281-291.

8 Burrell, David B. 1979. Aquinas: God and Action. Notre Dame, IN: University of Notre Dame Press.

9 Caillois, Roger. 1961. Man, Play, and Games. Trans. Meyer Barash. New York: Free Press.

10 Csikszentmihalyi, Mihaly. 1975. "Play and Intrinsic Rewards." Journal of Humanistic Psychology 15/3:41-63.

11 Daniels, Marilyn. 1981. The Dance in Christianity: A History

of Religious Dance Through the Ages. New York: Paulist
Press.

12 de Kleen, Tyra. 1970. Mudras: The Ritual Hand-Poses of
the Buddha Priests and the Shiva Priests of Bali. New Hyde
Park, NY: University Books.

13 De Rios, Marlene D., and Fred Katz. 1975. "Some Relationships Between Music and Hallucinogenic Ritual: The 'Jungle
Gym' in Consciousness." Ethos 3/1:64-76.

14 Devi, Ragini. 1972. Dance Dialects of India. Delhi & London:
International Publications Service.

15 Dorcy, Jean. 1961. The Mime. New York: R. Speller.

16 Dubs, Lindsay J. 1980. "Praise God with Timbrel and Dance."
Sojourners 9:26-27.

17 Emery, Lynne Fauley. 1980. Black Dance in the United States
from 1619-1970. New York: Books for Libraries.

18 Evanchuk, Robin. 1977-78. "Problems in Reconstructing a
Shaker Religious Dance Ritual." Journal of the Association
of Graduate Dance Ethnologists. UCLA I (Fall-Winter).

19 Eyman, F. 1964. "Lacrosse and the Cayuga Thunder Rite."
Expedition 6/4:14-19.

20 Fischer, Herbert. 1965. "Use of Gesture in Preparing Medica-
ments and in Healing." Trans. J. Adams. History of Religions 5:18-53.

21 Friedlander, Ira. 1975. The Whirling Dervishes. New York:
Macmillan.

22 Grimes, Ronald L. 1975. "Masking: Toward a Phenomenology
of Exteriorization." Journal of the American Academy of Religion 53:508-16.

23 Handelman, Don. 1977. "Play and Ritual: Complementary
Frames of Meta-Communication," in It's a Funny Thing, Hu-
mor. Eds. Antony J. Chapman and Hugh C. Foot. Oxford,
Eng.: Pergamon Press.

24 Hanna, Judith Lynne. 1979. "Dance in Religion." Ch. 5 of
her To Dance Is Human: A Theory of Nonverbal Communication. Austin, TX: University of Texas Press.

25 Harvey, B. 1972. "Work and Festa Ferianda in Medieval England." Journal of Ecclesiastical History 23:289-308.

26 Hospital, Clifford G. 1976-77. "Krsna and the Theology of Play." Studies in Religion/Sciences Religieuses 6/3:285-91.

27 Jellinek, E. M. 1977. "Symbolism of Drinking: A Culture-Historical Approach." Journal of Studies in Alcohol 38:849-66.

28 Kane, Cornelius T. 1978. Habit: A Theological and Psychological Analysis. Washington, DC: University Press of America.

29 Kaplan, Donald. 1971. "Gestures, Sensibilities, Scripts." Performance 1/1:31-46.

30 Kealiinohomoku, Joann W. 1981. "Dance as a Rite of Transformation," in Discourse in Ethnomusicology II. Ed. Caroline Card, et al. Bloomington: Indiana University Publications.

31 Kipnis, Claude. 1974. The Mime Book. New York: Harper & Row.

32 Kosuke, Koyama. 1981. "Ritual of Limping Dance: A Botanical Observation." Union Seminary Quarterly Review 36:91-104.

33 Lawler, Lillian B. 1964. The Dance in Ancient Greece. Iowa City: University of Iowa Press.

34 Lowenthal, I. 1978. "Ritual Performance and Religious Experience." Journal of Anthropological Research 34:392-414.

35 Luyster, Robert. 1977. "Myth, Mystery and Mysticism: The Dance of Dionysus and Shiva." Journal of the American Academy of Religion 45/3:901-32.

36 Macnair, P. L. 1973. "Kwakiutl Winter Dance, A Re-enactment." Artscanada 30:94-114.

37 Marks, Morton. 1974. "Uncovering Ritual Structures in Afro-American Music," in Religious Movements in Contemporary America. Ed. Zaretsky & Leone. Princeton: Princeton University Press.

38 Mead, George Herbert. 1967. Mind, Self, and Society. Chicago: University of Chicago Press.

39 _____. 1972. The Philosophy of the Act. Chicago: University of Chicago Press.

40 Midgett, D. K. 1977. "Performance Roles and Musical Change in a Caribbean Society." Ethnomusicology 21:55-73.

41 Munn, Nancy. 1973. "Symbolism in a Ritual Context: Aspects

of Symbolic Action," in Handbook of Social and Cultural Anthropology. Ed. John J. Honigmann. Chicago: Rand-
McNally.

42 Nebesky-Wojkowitz, Rene de. 1976. Tibetan Religious Dances.
The Hague: Mouton.

43 Ortegel, Adelaide. 1976. A Dancing People. West Lafayette,
IN: Center for Contemporary Celebration.

44 Quasten, Johannes. 1983. Music and Worship in Pagan and
Christian Antiquity. Trans. Boniface Ramsey. Washington,
DC: National Association of Pastoral Musicians.

45 Rahner, Hugo. 1967. Man at Play. New York: Herder.

46 Reed, Carlynn. 1978. And We Have Danced: A History of
the Sacred Dance Guild: 1958-78. Austin, TX: Sharing Co.

47 Rock, Judith. 1978. Theology in the Shape of Dance: Using
Dance in Worship and in Theological Process. Austin, TX:
Sharing Co.

48 Rossen, J. M. 1978. "Suahongi of Bellona: Polynesian Ritual
of Music." Ethnomusicology 22:397-439.

49 Royce, Anya Peterson. 1980. The Anthropology of Dance.
Bloomington: Indiana University Press.

50 Saunders, E. Dale. 1960. Mudra: A Study of Symbolic Gestures in Japanese Buddhist Sculpture. Princeton, NJ:
Princeton University Press.

51 Schechner, Richard. 1981. "Restoration of Behavior." Studies in the Anthropology of Visual Communication. 8:2-45.

52 _____, and Mady Schuman, eds. 1976. Ritual, Play, and
Performance: Readings in the Social Sciences/Theatre. New
York: Seabury.

53 Schmitt, J. C. L. 1982. The Symbolism of the Gesture. New
York: Harwood.

54 Smith, H. H. 1973. "Red Man Dances," North American Review 258:104-7.

55 Taylor, Margaret Fisk. 1976(a). Look Up and Live: Dance
in Prayer and Meditation. Austin, TX: Sharing Co.

56 _____. 1976(b). A Time to Dance: Symbolic Movement in
Worship. Austin, TX: Sharing Co.

57 Thompson, Robert Farris. 1974. African Art in Motion: Icon and Act. Berkeley: University of California Press.

58 Tucci, D. S. 1977. "High Mass as Sacred Dance." Theology Today 34:58-72.

59 Turner, Victor. 1982. From Ritual to Theatre: The Human Seriousness of Play. New York: Performing Arts.

60 Waggoner, G. 1977. "Dancing in a Pig Trough." Western Folklore 36:169-70.

61 Weakland, R. 1967. "Music and Liturgy in Evolution." Liturgical Arts 35:114-117.

62 Wembak-Rashid, J. A. R. 1971. "Isinyago and Midimu: Masked Dancers of Tanzania and Mozambique." African Arts 4/2:38-44.

63 Wosien, Maria-Gabriele. 1974. Sacred Dance: Encounter with the Gods. London: Thames and Hudson.

64 Wright, Derrick. 1975. "Musical Meaning and Its Social Determinant." Sociology 9/3:419-35.

1.2 SPACE
(Geography, Environment, Architecture, Shrines, Sacred Places)

65 Allmen, J. J. 1964. "A Short Theology of the Place of Worship." Studia Liturgica 3:156.

66 Anonymous. 1981. "American Amusement Parks." Journal of Popular Culture 15/1:56-179.

67 Ardener, Shirley, ed. 1981. Women and Space: Ground Rules and Social Maps. New York: St. Martin's Press.

68 Bachelard, Gaston. 1969. The Poetics of Space. Trans. Maria Jolas. Boston: Beacon.

69 Ballinger, Franchot. 1978. "Responsible Center: Man and Nature in Pueblo and Navaho Ritual Songs and Prayers." American Quarterly 30:90-107.

70- Bhardwaj, Surinder Mohan. 1973. Hindu Places of Pilgrimage
71   in India: A Study in Cultural Geography. Berkeley: University of California Press.

72 Bourdieu, P. 1973. "The Berber House," in Rules and Mean-
    ings. Ed. Mary Douglas. Harmondsworth, Eng.: Penguin.

73 Buttner, Manfred. 1975. "Religion and Geography." Numen
    21:163-96.

74 Christian, William A., Jr. 1977. "The Spanish Shrine."
    Numen 24:72-78.

75 Clampet, M. K. 1970. "Nature as a Sacred Symbol in Religious-
    ly Oriented Summer Camps." Journal for the Scientific Study
    of Religion 9:151-52.

76 Cohn, Robert L. 1981. The Shape of Sacred Space: Four
    Biblical Studies. Chico, CA: Scholars Press.

77 Dougherty, James. 1980. The Fivesquare City: The City in
    the Religious Imagination. Notre Dame, IN: Notre Dame
    University Press.

78 Du Toit, Brian M., ed. 1977. Drugs, Rituals and Altered
    States of Consciousness. Rotterdam: A. A. Balkema.

79 Eck, Diana L. 1982. Banaras: City of Light. New York:
    Knopf.

80 Fox, Richard. 1977. "Regal-Ritual Cities," in his Urban An-
    thropology: Cities in Their Cultural Setting. Englewood
    Cliffs, NJ: Prentice-Hall.

81 Gossen, Gary H. 1974. Chamulas in the World of the Sun:
    Time and Space in a Maya Oral Tradition. Cambridge, MA:
    Harvard University Press.

82 Graber, Linda. 1976. Wilderness as Sacred Space. Washing-
    ton, DC: Association of American Geographers.

83 Grapard, Allan G. 1982. "Flying Mountains and Walkers of
    Emptiness: Toward a Definition of Sacred Space in Japanese
    Religion." History of Religions 20/3:195-221.

84 Green, Arthur. 1977. "Zaddiq as Axis Mundi in Later Juda-
    ism." Journal of the American Academy of Religion 45:327-47.

85 Greenwood, N. H., and C. W. White. 1970. "Mogollon Ritual:
    A Spatial Configuration of a Non-Village Pattern." Archaeol-
    ogy 23:298-301.

86 Gutschow, N. 1977. "Ritual as Mediator of Space: Kathman-
    du." Ekistics 44:309-12.

87 Hammond, Peter. 1961. Liturgy and Architecture. New
    York: Columbia University Press.

88 Haran, Menahem. 1978. Temples and Temple-Service in An-
    cient Israel: An Inquiry into the Character of Cult Phenom-
    ena and the Historical Setting of the Priestly School. New
    York: Oxford University Press.

89 Hart, Ray. 1973. "The Poiesis of Place." Journal of Reli-
    gion 53:36-47.

90 Hiller, Carl E. 1974. Cave to Cathedrals: Architecture of
    the World's Great Religions. Boston: Little, Brown.

91 Indinopulos. T. A. 1978. "Jerusalem the Blessed: The
    Shrines of Three Faiths." Christian Century 95:386-91.

92 Irwin, John. 1982. "The Sacred Anthill and the Cult of the
    Primordial Mound." History of Religions 21/4:339-60.

93 James, E. O. 1965. From Cave to Cathedral: Temples and
    Shrines of Prehistoric, Classical, and Early Christian Times.
    London: Thames and Hudson.

94 Janzen, W. 1973. "Geography of Faith: A Christian Per-
    spective on the Meaning of Places." Studies in Religion/
    Sciences Religieuses 3/2:166-82.

95 Jung, L. Shannon. 1982. "Spatiality, Relativism, and Author-
    ity." Journal of the American Academy of Religion 50/2:
    215-235.

96 Kaplan, Donald M. 1968. "Theatre Architecture: A Deriva-
    tion of the Primal Cavity." The Drama Review 12/3:105-16.

97 Keyes, Charles F. 1975. "Buddhist Pilgrimage Centers and
    the Twelve-Year Cycle: Northern Thai Moral Orders in
    Space and Time." History of Religions 15:71-89.

98 Kitahara, M. 1974. "Living Quarter Arrangements in Polyga-
    my and Circumcision and Segregation of Males at Puberty."
    Ethnology 13:401-13.

99 Kliever, Lonnie. 1977. "Story and Space: The Forgotten
    Dimension." Journal of the American Academy of Religion
    45/2:529-563.

100 Klimkeit, Hans J. 1975. "Spatial Orientation in Mythical
    Thinking as Exemplified in Ancient Egypt: Considerations
    Toward a Geography of Religions." History of Religions
    14:266-81.

101 Littlejohn, J. 1963. "Temne Space." Anthropological Quar-
     terly 36/1:1-17.

102 Lodrick, Deryck O. 1981. Sacred Cows, Sacred Places: Ori-
     gins and Survivals of Animal Homes in India. Berkeley:
     University of California Press.

103 McAllester, David P., and Susan W. McAllester. 1980.
     Hogans: Navajo Houses and House Songs. New York:
     Columbia University Press.

104 McDonnell, K., and C. Meinberg. 1965. "Architecture and
     the Constitution in the Sacred Liturgy." Liturgical Arts
     34:2-6.

105 Marshall, L. 1973. "Each Side of the Fire," in Rules and
     Meanings. Ed. Mary Douglas. Harmondsworth, Eng.:
     Penguin.

106 Michell, George. 1977. The Hindu Temple: An Introduction
     to Its Meaning and Forms. London: Paul Elek.

107 Mudiraj, G. N. R. 1973. "Spatial Differentiation of Castes:
     Analysis of a Regional Pattern." Man in India 53/1:13-18.

108 Muller, J. C. 1976. "Replication, Scission, and Territory
     Among the Rukuba (Nigeria)." Anthropos 71/5-6:738-67.

109 Nakashima, M. 1966. "Church Architecture in Japan and
     the Impact of the Liturgy." Liturgical Arts 35:13-18.

110 Nerlich, Graham. 1976. The Shape of Space. New York:
     Cambridge University Press.

111 Nitschke, G. 1973. "Patterns of Renewal (Japan)." Archi-
     tectural Design 43/3:151-3.

112 _____. 1974. "Shrine: An Investigation into the Origin
     of, and the Relationships Between, Human Building, Sign-
     Systems and Religious Beliefs in East Asia." Architectural
     Design 44/12:748-91.

113 Ong, Walter J. 1969. "World as View and World as Event."
     American Anthropologist 71:634-47.

114 Pavia, R. P. 1966. "Building the New Jerusalem." Liturgi-
     cal Arts 34:140-2.

115 Perin, Constance. 1977. Everything in Its Place: Social
     Order and Land Use in America. Princeton, NJ: Princeton
     University Press.

116 Quantrill, Malcolm. 1974. Ritual and Response in Architecture.
     London: Lund Humphries.

117- Ray, Benjamin. 1977. "Sacred Space and Royal Shrines in
118 Buganda." History of Religions 16:363-73.

119 Richardson, K. P. 1977. "Polliwogs and Shillbacks: An
     Analysis of the Equator Crossing Ritual." Western Folklore
     36:154-9.

120 Rubenstein, R. L. 1970. "The Cave, the Rock, and the
     Tent: The Meaning of Place in Contemporary America," in
     his Morality and Eros. New York: McGraw-Hill.

121 Sack, R. D. 1976. "Magic and Space." Association of Amer-
     ican Geographers Annals 66:309-22.

122 Sharma, Ursula. 1974. "Public Shrines and Private Interests:
     The Symbolism of the Village Temple." Sociological Bulletin
     23/1:71-92.

123 Shiner, L. E. 1972. "Sacred Space, Profane Space, Human
     Space." Journal of the American Adademy of Religion
     40:425-36.

124 Simson, Otto von. 1964. The Gothic Cathedral. New York:
     Harper & Row.

125 Smith, Jonathan Z. 1978(a). "The Wobbling Pivot," in his
     Map Is Not Territory. Leiden: Brill.

126 _____. 1978(b). "Earth and Gods," in his Map Is Not Ter-
     ritory. Leiden: Brill.

127 _____. 1978(c). "The Influence of Symbols on Social
     Change," in his Map Is Not Territory. Leiden: Brill.

128 Sovik, E. A. 1973. "Sacrality, Place and Symbol." Worship
     47:547-51.

129 Stookey, L. H. 1969. "Gothic Cathedral as the Heavenly
     Jerusalem: Liturgical and Theological Sources." Gesta
     8/1:35-40.

130 Strong, John S. 1977. "Gandhakuti: The Perfumed Chamber
     of the Buddha." History of Religions 16:390-406.

131 Tuan, Yi-Fu. 1974. Topophilia: A Study of Environmental
     Perception, Attitudes and Values. Englewood Cliffs, NJ:
     Prentice-Hall.

132 _____. 1976. "Geopiety: A Theme in Man's Attachment to Nature and Place," in Geographies of the Mind: Essays in Historical Geosophy in Honor of John Kirkland Wright. Ed. David Lowenthal and Martyn J. Bowden. New York: Oxford University Press.

133 _____. 1977. Space and Place: The Perspective of Experience. Minneapolis: University of Minnesota Press.

134 Turner, Harold. 1979. From Temple to Meeting House: The Phenomenology and Theology of Places of Worship. The Hague: Mouton.

135 Wheatley, Paul. 1969. City as Symbol. London: H. K. Lewis.

136 _____. 1971. The Pivot of the Four Quarters: A Preliminary Enquiry into the Origins and Character of the Ancient Chinese City. Chicago: Aldine.

137 White, James F. 1978. "Liturgy and the Language of Space." Worship 52:57-66.

138 Wolf, Herbert C. 1978. "Linga as Center: A Study in Religious Phenomenology." Journal of the American Academy of Religion 46:365.

139 Young, Katherine K. 1980. "Tirtha and the Metaphor of Crossing Over." Studies in Religion/Sciences Religieuses 9/1:61-68.

140 Zeitlin, S. 1961. "Temple and Worship." Jewish Quarterly Review 51:209-41.

1.3 TIME
(Season, Holiday, Repetition, Calendar)

141 Adam, A. 1981. The Liturgical Year. New York: Pueblo.

142 Andreasen, N. E. 1974. "Recent Studies of the Old Testament Sabbath: Some Observations." Zeitschrift für die Alttestamentliche Wissenschaft 86/4:453-69.

143 Barnes, A. J. 1971. "Time Flies Like an Arrow." Man (N.S.) 6:537-52.

144 Beane, W. C. 1973. "Cosmological Structure of Mythical Time: Kali-Sakti." History of Religions 13:54-83.

145 Beckwith, R. T. 1971. "Qumran Calendar and the Sacrifices
     of the Essenes." Revue de Qumran 7/4:587-91.

146 Collins, A. C. 1973-74. "The Yearbearer Ceremonies of Yuc-
     atan and Highland Guatemala." Human Mosaic 7/1:1-8.

147 Denis-Boulet, Noele M. 1960. The Christian Calendar. New
     York: Hawthorn.

148 Driver, Tom F. 1960. The Sense of History in Greek and
     Shakespearean Drama. New York: Columbia University
     Press.

149 Ducey, Michael H. 1977. Sunday Morning: Aspects of Urban
     Ritual. New York: Free Press.

150 Evans-Pritchard, E. E. 1973. "Time Is Not a Continuum," in
     Rules and Meanings. Ed. Mary Douglas. Harmondsworth, Eng.:
     Penguin.

151 Hickling, Colin J. A. 1977. "Eucharist and Time." Theology
     80:197-204.

152 Horst, R. 1979. "Ritual Time Regained in Zorilla's Don Juan
     Tenario." Romantic Review 70:80-93.

153 Ingham, John M. 1971. "Time and Space in Ancient Mexico:
     The Symbolic Dimensions of Clanship." Man (N.S.) 6:615-29.

154 Johnson, David. 1977. "The Wisdom of Festival (Akitu:
     Babylonian New Year)." Parabola 2/2:20-3.

155 Kalokyris, K. D. 1967. "Byzantine Iconography and Liturgi-
     cal Time." Eastern Churches Review 1:359-63.

156 Lee, Bernard J. 1978. "The Sacrament of Creative Transfor-
     mation." Process Studies 8:240-52.

157 Lester, D., and A. T. Beck. 1975. "Suicide and National
     Holidays." Psychological Reports 36:52.

158 Luce, Gay Gaer. 1971. Body Time: Physiological Rhythms
     and Social Stress. New York: Pantheon Books.

159 Neumann, Frankie J. 1975. "The Dragon and the Dog: Two
     Symbols of Time in Nahuatl Religion." Numen 22:1-23.

160 Ozouf, M. 1975. "Space and Time in the Festivals of the
     French Revolution." Comparative Studies in Society and
     History 17:372-84.

161 Sackett, Lee. 1977. "Confronting the Dreamtime: Belief and
     Symbolism in an Aboriginal Ritual." Ethnos 42/3:156-79.

162 Schauss, Hayim. 1962. Guide to Jewish Holy Days. Trans.
     Samuel Jaffe. New York: Schocken.

163 Segal, J. B. 1961. "Hebrew Festivals and the Calendar."
     Journal of Semitic Studies 6:74-94.

164 Soberg, Winton. 1977. Redeem the Time: The Puritan Sab-
     bath in Early America. Cambridge, MA: Harvard University
     Press.

165 Taft, Robert. 1981. "The Liturgical Year." Worship 55:11-23.

166 Wigley, John. 1980. The Rise and Fall of the Victorian Sun-
     day. Manchester, Eng.: Manchester University Press.

167 Wolowelsky, J. B. 1972. "On Iyyar's Holidays." Judaism
     21:299-302.

168 Woodward, John A. 1968. "The Anniversary: A Contemporary
     Diegueno Complex." Ethnology 7/1:86-94.

169 Zerubavel, Eviar. 1981. Hidden Rhythms: Schedules and
     Calendars in Social Life. Chicago: University of Chicago
     Press.

1.4 OBJECTS
(Masks, Costumes, Fetishes, Icons, Art)

170 Anonymous. 1972. Image and Identity: The Role of Masks
     in Various Cultures. Los Angeles: Museum of Cultural
     History Galleries, UCLA.

171 Benes, Peter. 1977. The Masks of Orthodoxy: Folk Grave-
     stone Carving in Plymouth County, Massachusetts. Amherst:
     University of Massachusetts Press.

172 Bethe, Monica. 1978. Bugaku Masks. New York: Kodansha.

173 Biebuyck, D. P. 1974. "Mumbira: Musical Instrument of a
     Nyanga Initiation." African Arts 7/4:42-5.

174 Blau, Harold. 1966. "Function and False Faces." Journal of
     American Folklore 79.

175- Bonifazi, Conrad. 1967. A Theology of Things. Philadelphia:
176   Lippincott.

177 Brandon, Samuel G. F. 1975. Man and God in Art and Ritual: A Study of Iconography, Architecture and Ritual Action as Primary Evidence of Religious Belief and Practice. New York: Scribners.

178 Child, Heather, and Dorothy Colles. 1971. Christian Symbols, Ancient and Modern: A Handbook for Students. New York: Scribners.

179 Deming, Robert H. 1975. Ceremony and Art: Robert Herrick's Poetry. The Hague: Mouton.

180 Didron, Adolphe Napoleon. 1965. Christian Iconography. Trans. E. J. Millington. New York: Ungar.

181 Drewal, H. J. 1974. "Gelede Masquerade: Imagery and Motif." African Arts 7/4:8-19.

182 Elder, J. L., and D. R. Pederson. 1978. "Preschool Children's Use of Objects in Symbolic Play." Child Development 49:500-4.

183 Errington, Frederick Karl. 1974. Karavar: Masks and Power in a Melanesian Ritual. Ithaca, NY: Cornell University Press.

184 Eyo, E. 1974. "Abua Masquerades." African Arts 7/2:52-5.

185 Falk, Nancy. 1977. "To Gaze on the Sacred Traces." History of Religions 16:281-93.

186 Furst, Peter, et al. 1973-74. "Stones, Bones and Skin: Ritual and Shamanic Art." Artscanada nos. 184-87.

187 Galavaris, George. 1981. The Icon in the Life of the Church. Leiden: Brill.

188 Goethals, Gregor. 1975. "Images and Values: Notes on Some Relationships Between 'Museum' and 'Street' Images." Journal of Popular Culture 9/2:471-79.

189 Goldstein, M. 1977. "Ceremonial Role of the Maya Flanged Censer." Man 12:405-20.

190 Gutmann, Joseph, ed. 1977. The Images and the Word: Confrontations in Judaism, Christianity and Islam. Chico, CA: Scholars Press.

191 Halpin, Marjorie M., and Michael M. Ames, eds. 1980. Manlike Monsters on Trial: Early Records and Modern Evidence. Vancouver, BC: University of British Columbia Press.

50   Part 1: Ritual Components

192 Haran, M. 1960. "Uses of Incense in the Ancient Israelite Ritual." Vetus Testamentum 10:113-29.

193 Harvey, Byron. 1970. Ritual in Pueblo Art. New York: Museum of the American Indian.

194 Hawthorn, Audrey. 1967. Art of the Kwakiutl Indians. Seattle: University of Washington Press.

195 Honigmann, J. J. 1977. "The Masked Face." Ethos 5/3: 263-80.

196 King, J. C. H. 1979. Portrait Masks from the Northwest Coast of America. London: Thames and Hudson.

197 Kippenberg, H. G., ed. 1982. Visible Religion: Annual for Religious Iconography. Leiden: Brill.

198 Lesko, David S. 1978. "Art and Liturgy: The Fixing of a Thesis." St. Vladimir's Theological Quarterly 22/2-3:127-40.

199 Lommel, Andreas. 1972. Masks: Their Meaning and Function. New York: McGraw-Hill.

200 Ludwig, Allan I. 1966. Graven Images: New England Stonecarving and Its Symbols, 1650-1815. Middletown, CT: Wesleyan University Press.

201 Marshall, W. L. 1974. "Combined Treatment Approach to the Reduction of Multiple Fetish-Related Behaviors." Journal of Consulting and Clinical Psychology 42:613-16.

202 Monti, Franco. 1969. African Masks. London: Paul Hamlyn.

203 Munn, Nancy D. 1973. Walbiri Iconography: Graphic Representation and Cultural Australian Society. Ithaca, NY: Cornell University Press.

204 Murray, Joan. 1980. "New Rites: Irland and Mordowanec." Artsmagazine 12/50:31-4.

205 Neumann, F. J. 1973. "Paper, a Sacred Material in Aztec Ritual." History of Religions 13:149-59.

206 Ojo, J. R. O. 1978. "Symbolism and Significance of Epa-Type Masquerade Headpieces." Man 13:455-70.

207 Ouspensky, Leonid. 1978. Theology of the Icon. Crestwood, NY: St. Vladimir's Seminary Press.

208 Palmer, K. 1977. "Myth, Ritual and Rock Art." Archaeology and Physical Anthropology in Oceania 12:38-50.

209 Pellegrino, M. 1968. "Art and the Liturgy." Liturgical Arts
     36:65-9.

210 Picton, J. 1974. "Masks and the Igbirra." African Arts
     7/2:38-41.

211 Ranoff, F. 1970. "Food and Faeces: A Melanesian Rite."
     Man (N.S.) 5:237-52.

212 Rawson, Philip. 1973. The Art of Tantra. Greenwich, CT:
     New York Graphic Society.

213 Ray, Dorothy Jean. 1967. Eskimo Masks: Art and Ceremony.
     Vancouver: J. J. Douglas.

214 Regan, Patrick. 1978. "Veneration of the Cross." Worship
     52:2-12.

215 Renwick Gallery. 1982. Celebration: A World of Art and
     Ritual. Washington, DC: Smithsonian.

216 Rubens, Alfred. 1981. A History of Jewish Costume.
     London: Peter Owen.

217 Shalleck, Jamie. 1973. Masks. New York: Viking.

218 Stark, Louisa R. 1972. "The Origin of the Penitente 'Death
     Cart.'" Journal of American Folklore 84:304-10.

219 Volavkova, Z. 1972. "Nkisi Figures of the Lower Congo."
     African Arts 5/2:52-9.

220 Warren, D. M. 1975. "Bono Royal Regalia." African Arts
     8/2:16-21.

221 Weil, Peter M. 1971. "The Masked Figure and Social Control:
     The Mandinka Case." Africa 41:4.

222 Wells, L. T. 1977. "Harley Masks of Northeast Liberia."
     African Arts 10:22-7.

223 Zahan, D. 1975. "Colors and Body Painting in Black Africa:
     The Problem of the Half-Man." Diogenes 90:100-19.

1.5 SYMBOL, METAPHOR

224 Babcock, Barbara A. 1978. "Too Many, Too Few: Ritual
     Modes of Signification." Semiotica 23/3-4:291-301.

225 Beck, Brenda. 1978. "The Metaphor as a Mediator Between
     Semantic and Analogic Modes of Thought." Current An-
     thropology 19/1:83-97.

226 Bock, E. W. 1966. "Symbols in Conflict: Official Versus
     Folk Religion." Journal for the Scientific Study of Religion
     5:204-12.

227 Cohen, Abner. 1979. "Political Symbolism." The Annual
     Review of Anthropology 8:87-113.

228 Crumrine, N. R. 1970. "Ritual Drama and Culture Change."
     Comparative Studies in Social History 12/4:361-72.

229 Duncan, Hugh Dalziel. 1968. Symbols of Society. London:
     Oxford University Press.

230 Eco, Umberto. 1982. "On Symbols." Semiotic Inquiry 2/1:
     15-44.

231 Ferguson, George. 1966. Signs and Symbols in Christian
     Art. New York: Oxford University Press.

232 Fernandez, J. 1974. "Mission of Metaphor in Expressive
     Culture." Current Anthropology 15:119-45.

233 _____. "The Performance of Ritual Metaphors." Ch. 4 in
     The Social Use of Metaphor: Essays on the Anthropology
     of Rhetoric. Eds. J. David Sapir and J. Christopher
     Crocker. Philadelphia: University of Pennsylvania Press.

234 Firth, Raymond. 1973. Symbols: Public and Private.
     Ithaca, NY: Cornell University Press.

235 Greeley, Andrew. 1961. "Myths, Symbols and Rituals in the
     Modern World." The Critic 20:3.

236 Grieder, T. 1975. "Interpretation of Ancient Symbols."
     American Anthropologist 77:849-55.

237 Hardwick, Charley D. 1977. "Ironic Culture and Polysym-
     bolic Religiosity." Theologische Zeitschrift 33:283-93.

238 Hayley, Audrey. 1968. "Symbolic Equations: The Ox and
     the Cucumber." Man (N.S.) 3:262-71.

239 Hill, Carole E., ed. 1975. Symbols and Society: Essays on
     Belief Systems in Action. Athens, GA: Southern Anthro-
     pological Society.

240 Jarvie, I. C. 1976. "On the Limits of Symbolic Interpretation
     in Anthropology." Current Anthropology 17:687-701.

Symbol, Metaphor (1.5)   53

241 Katz, P., and F. E. Katz. 1977. "Symbols as Charters in
     Cultural Change: The Jewish Case." Anthropos 72/3-4:
     486-96.

242 Kliever, Lonnie D. 1979. "Polysymbolism and Modern Reli-
     giosity." Journal of Religion 59:169-94.

243 Lamphere, Louise. 1969. "Symbolic Elements in Navajo Rit-
     ual." Southwestern Journal of Anthropology 25:279-305.

244 Miller, S. H. 1968. "Liturgy: Sign and Symbol." Una Sancta
     25/1:41-52.

245 Munn, Nancy D. 1973. "Symbolism in a Ritual Context: As-
     pects of Symbolic Action," in Handbook of Social and Cultural
     Anthropology. Ed. John J. Honigman. Chicago: Rand-
     McNally.

246 Obeyesekere, Gananath. 1981. Medusa's Hair: An Essay on
     Personal Symbols and Religious Experience. Chicago: Uni-
     versity of Chicago Press.

247 Ortner, S. B. 1973. "On Key Symbols." American Anthro-
     pologist 75:1338-46.

248 Pemberton, J. 1977. "Cluster of Sacred Symbols: Orisa
     Worship Among the Igbomina Yoruba of Ila-Orangun." His-
     tory of Religions 17:1-28.

249 Poulsen, Richard C. 1982. The Pure Experience of Order:
     Essays on the Symbolic in the Folk Material Culture of
     Western America. Albuquerque: University of New Mexico
     Press.

250 Rigby, Peter. 1966. "Dual Symbolic Classification Among the
     Gogo of Central Tanzania." Africa 36:1-16.

251 Sandner, Donald. 1979. Navaho Symbols of Healing. New
     York: Harcourt Brace Jovanovich.

252 Skorupski, John. 1976. Symbol and Theory. Cambridge,
     Eng.: Cambridge University Press.

253 Sperber, Dan. 1975. Rethinking Symbolism. Trans. Alice L.
     Morton. Cambridge, Eng.: Cambridge University Press.

254 Turner, V. W. 1967. The Forest of Symbols. Ithaca, NY:
     Cornell University Press.

255 _____. 1968. "Myth and Symbol," in International Ency-
     clopedia of Social Sciences. Ed. David Sills. London:
     Macmillan.

54   Part 1: Ritual Components

256   _____. 1973. "Symbols in African Ritual." Science
       179/4078:1100-05.

257   _____. 1974. Dramas, Fields and Metaphors: Symbolic
       Action in Human Society. Ithaca, NY: Cornell University
       Press.

258   _____. 1975. "Symbolic Studies," in Annual Review of
       Anthropology. Vol. 4. Ed. Bernard J. Siegel et al. Palo
       Alto, CA: Annual Reviews.

259   Wieting, S. G. 1972. "Myth and Symbolic Analysis of Claude
       Levi-Strauss and Victor Turner." Social Compass 19/2:
       139-54.

260   Zuckerkandl, Victor. 1973. Sound and Symbol: Music and
       the External World. Princeton, NJ: Princeton University
       Press.

1.6 GROUP
(Role, Kinship, Class, Caste, Family,
Hierarchy, Ethnicity, Acculturation)

261   Albrecht, Ruth. 1962. "The Role of Older People in Family
       Rituals," in Social and Psychological Aspects of Aging: Ag-
       ing Around the World. Ed. Clark Tibbits and Wilma Dona-
       hue. New York: Columbia University Press.

262   Beattie, John. 1966. "Ritual and Social Change." Man 1/1:
       60-73.

263   Befu, Harumi. 1964. "Ritual Kinship in Japan: Its Variabil-
       ity and Resiliency." Sociologus 14/2:150-68.

264   Canetti, Elias. 1978. Crowds and Power. New York: Sea-
       bury.

265   Chock, P. P. 1974. "Time, Nature and Spirit: A Symbolic
       Analysis of Greek-American Spiritual Kinship." American
       Ethnologist 1:33-47.

266   Cohen, Yehudi. 1964. "The Establishment of Identity in a
       Social Nexus: The Special Case of Initiation Ceremonies and
       Their Relation to Value and Legal Systems." American An-
       thropologist 3/1:529-52.

267   Crumrine, N. R. 1976. "Mediating Roles in Ritual and Sym-
       bolism: Northwest Mexico and the Pacific Northwest."
       Anthropologica 18/2:131-52.

268 Davis, R. 1974. "Tolerance and Intolerance of Ambiguity in
     Northern Thai Myth and Ritual." Ethnology 13:1-24.

269 Dewey, Alice G. 1970. "Ritual as a Mechanism for Urban
     Adaptation." Man 5/3:438-48.

270 Dewhirst, J. 1976. "Coast Salish Summer Festivals: Rituals
     for Upgrading Social Identity." Anthropologica 18/2:231-73.

271 Eder, J. F. 1977. "Modernization, Deculturation and Social
     Structural Stress: The Disappearance of the Umbay Cere-
     mony Among the Batak of the Philippines." Mankind 11/2:
     144-9.

272 Freeman, Susan Tax. 1968. "Religious Aspects of the Social
     Organization of a Castilian Village." American Anthropologist
     70/1:34-49.

273 Frundt, Henry J. 1969. "Rite Involvement and Community
     Formation." Sociological Analysis 30/2:91-107.

274 Galt, Anthony H. 1973. "Carnival on the Island Pantelleria:
     Ritualized Community Solidarity in an Atomistic Society."
     Ethnology 12/3:325-40.

275 Goldberg, H. E. 1978. "Mimuna and the Minority Status of
     Moroccan Jews." Ethnology 17:75-87.

276 Goode, William J. 1978. The Celebration of Heroes: Prestige
     as a Control System. Berkeley: University of California
     Press.

277 Hage, P. 1979. "Symbolic Culinary Mediation: A Group
     Model." Man 14:81-92.

278 Hobsbawn, E. J. 1965. "Ritual in Social Movements," in his
     Primitive Rebels: Studies in Archaic Forms of Social Move-
     ment in the 19th and 20th Centuries. New York: Norton.

279 Ivey, S. K. 1977. "Ascribed Ethnicity and the Ethnic Dis-
     play Event: The Melungeons of Hancock County, Tennessee."
     Western Folklore 36:85-107.

280 Jay, Edward. 1964. "Structural Obstacles to Tribal Accultura-
     tion: The Case of Regional Ceremonial Integration in Bastar."
     Eastern Anthropologist 18/3:159-64.

281 Kennedy. J. G., and H. Fahim. 1974. "Nubian Dhikr Rituals
     and Cultural Change." The Muslim World 64:205-19.

282 Knittel, R. E. 1974. "Essential and Non-Essential Ritual in
     Programs of Planned Change." Human Organization 33:394-7.

56   Part 1:   Ritual Components

283 Levy, Janet E. 1981. "Religious Ritual and Social Stratifica-
    tion in Prehistoric Societies: An Example from Bronze Age
    Denmark." History of Religions 21/2:172-88.

284 Liebman, S. B. 1975. "Sephardic Ethnicity in the Spanish
    New World Colonies." Jewish Social Studies 37:141-62.

285 Lueschen, Guenther, et al. 1971. "Family Organization,
    Interaction and Ritual: A Cross-Cultural Study in Bulgaria,
    Finland, Germany, and Ireland." Journal of Marriage and
    the Family 33/1:228-34.

286 _____. 1972. "Family, Ritual and Secularization: A Cross-
    National Study Conducted in Bulgaria, Finland, Germany and
    Ireland." Social Compass 19/4:519-36.

287 Malewska, Hanna E. 1961. "Religious Ritualism, Rigid Ethics,
    and Severity in Upbringing." Polish Sociological Bulletin
    1-2:71-8.

288 Michaelson, Evalyn J., and Walter Goldschmidt. 1976. "Fam-
    ily and Land in Peasant Ritual." American Ethnologist
    3/1:87-96.

289 Nutini, Hugo G., and Betty Bell. 1980. Ritual Kinship.
    Princeton, NJ: Princeton University Press.

290 Orenstein, Henry. 1965. "The Structure of Hindu Caste
    Values: A Preliminary Study of Hierarchy and Ritual De-
    filement." Ethnology 4/1:1-15.

291 Owens, Bill. 1975. Our Kind of People: American Groups
    and Rituals. Livermore, CA: Working Press.

292 Perinbanayagam, Robert S. 1965. "Caste, Religion and Rit-
    ual in Ceylon." Anthropological Quarterly 38/4:218-25.

293 Petersen, David L. 1977. "Covenant Ritual: A Tradio-
    Historical Perspective." Biblical Research 22:7-18.

294 Phillips, D. P., and K. A. Feldman. 1973. "A Dip in Deaths
    Before Ceremonial Occasions: Some New Relationships Be-
    tween Social Integration and Mortality." American Socio-
    logical Review 38/6:678-96.

295 Plotkin, V. 1978. "Ritual Coordination and Symbolic Repre-
    sentation in Primitive Society: The Evolution of Kinship."
    Dialectical Anthropology 3/4:279-314.

296 Rieck, J. 1974. "Fictive Parent-Child Relations in Japanese
    Religion." Journal of Comparative Family Studies 5/2:88-97.

297 Rosaldo, Renato I., Jr. 1968. "Metaphors of Hierarchy in a Mayan Ritual." American Anthropologist 70/3:524-36.

298 Saler, Benson. 1962. "Migration and Ceremonial Ties Among the Maya." Southwestern Journal of Anthropology 18/4:336-40.

299 Schlesinger, B. 1974. "The Jewish Family and Religion." Journal of Comparative Family Studies 5/2:27-36.

300 Schwartz, Barton M. 1964. "Ritual Aspects of Caste in Trinidad." Anthropological Quarterly 37/1:1-15.

301 Seneviratne, H. L. 1976. "Aristocrats and Rituals in Contemporary Ceylon." Journal of Asian and African Studies 11:97-101.

302 Sertel, Ayse K. 1971. "Ritual Kinship in Eastern Turkey." Anthropological Quarterly 44/1:37-50.

303 Slater, Philip. 1966. Microcosm: Structural, Psychological and Religious Evolution in Groups. New York: John Wiley.

304 Smith, David H. 1972. "Ritual in Voluntary Associations." Journal of Voluntary Action Research 1/4:39-53.

305 Swetnam, J. 1978. "Class-Based Community-Based Ritual Organization in Latin America." Ethnology 17:425-38.

306 Tooker, Elisabeth. 1968. "Masking and Matrilineality in North America." American Anthropologist 70/6:1170-75.

307 Tuck, D. R. 1976. "Santal Religion: Self Identification and Socialization in the Sohrae-Harvest Festival." Man in India 56/3:215-36.

308 Turner, V. W. 1972. "Passages, Margins, and Poverty: Religious Symbols of Communitas." Worship 46:390-412, 482-94.

309 Von Allmen, et al. 1981. Roles in the Liturgical Assembly. Trans. M. J. O'Connell. New York: Pueblo.

310 Wadley, S. S. 1976. "Brothers, Husbands, and Sometimes Sons: Kinsmen in North India Ritual." The Eastern Anthropologist 29/2:149-70.

311 Weisman, Ronald F. E. 1982. Ritual Brotherhood in Renaissance Florence. New York: Academic Press.

312 Wolin, S. J., et al. 1979. "Family Rituals and the Recurrence

of Alcoholism over Generations." American Journal of Psychiatry 136/4-8:589-93.

313 Wyllie, Robert W. 1968. "Ritual and Social Change: A
Ghanaian Example." American Anthropologist 70/1:21-33.

314 Young, L. C., and S. R. Ford. 1977. "God Is Society:
The Religious Dimension of Maoism." Sociological Inquiry
47/2:89-97.

1.7 SELF
(Body, Feeling, States of Consciousness, Gender)

315 Babcock, Barbara A. 1980. "Reflexivity: Definitions and
Discriminations." Semiotica 30/1-2:1-14.

316 Beidelman, T. O. 1961. "Right and Left Hand Among the
Kaguru: A Note on Symbolic Classification." Africa 31:
250-57.

317 _____. 1964. "Pig (Guluwe): An Essay on Ngulu Sexual
Symbolism and Ceremony." Southwestern Journal of Anthropology 20/4:359-92.

318 Bloomer, Kent C., and Charles W. Moore. 1977. Body, Memory and Architecture. New Haven, CT: Yale University
Press.

319 Bottomley, Frank. 1979. Attitudes to the Body in Western
Christendom. London: Lepus Books.

320 Brown, Judith K. 1963. "A Crosscultural Study of Female
Initiation Rites." American Anthropologist 65:837-53.

321 Burnshaw, Stanley. 1970. The Seamless Web. New York:
Braziller.

322 Collins, John J. 1969. "Transformations of the Self and
Duplication of Ceremonial Structure." International Journal
of Comparative Sociology 10/3-4:302-07.

323 Crocker, J. C. 1977. "Mirrored Self: Identity and Ritual
Inversion Among the Eastern Bororo." Ethnology 16:129-45.

324 Dange, Sadashiv Ambadas. 1979. Sexual Symbolism from the
Vedic Ritual. Delhi: Ajanta.

325 Davis, Charles. 1976. Body as Spirit. New York: Seabury.

Self (1.7)   59

326 Douglas, Mary. 1971. "Do Dogs Laugh? A Cross-Cultural
     Approach to Body Symbolism." Journal of Psychosomatic
     Research 15/4:387-90.

327 _____. 1982. Natural Symbols: Explorations in Cosmology.
     New York: Pantheon Books.

328 Ekman, Paul, and W. Friesen. 1975. Unmasking the Face.
     New York: Prentice-Hall.

329 El-Islam, M. F. 1967. "The Psychotherapeutic Bases of
     Some Arab Rituals." International Journal of Social Psy-
     chiatry 13/4:265-8.

330 Feldman, Sandor S. 1969. Mannerisms of Speech and Gestures
     in Everyday Life. New York: International Universities
     Press.

331 Feldstein, Leonard C. 1976. "The Human Body as Rhythm
     and Symbol: A Study in Practical Hermeneutics." The
     Journal of Medicine and Philosophy 1/2:136-61.

332 Fernandez, James W. 1980. "Reflections on Looking in Mir-
     rors." Semiotica 30/1-2:27-39.

333 Gager, John G. 1982. "Body-Symbols and Social Reality:
     Resurrection, Incarnation and Asceticism in Early Christian-
     ity." Religion 12:345-63.

334 Gay, Volney. 1980. "Death Anxiety in Modern and Pre-
     Modern Ritual." American Imago 37/2:180-214.

335 Harding, M. Esther. 1971. Woman's Mysteries Ancient and
     Modern: A Psychological Interpretation of the Feminine
     Principle as Portrayed in Myth, Story, and Dreams. New
     York: Harper & Row.

336 Hoch-Smith, Judith, and Anita Spring. 1978. Women in Rit-
     ual and Symbolic Roles. New York: Plenum.

337 Hosken, F. P. 1977-78. "Female Circumcision in Africa."
     Victimology 2/3-4:487-98.

338 Ishida, T. H. 1979. "Ego Adaptive Functions of Ritual."
     Dissertation Abstracts International 39/7-8:3518-19.

339 Just, P. 1972. "Men, Women and Mukanda: A Transforma-
     tional Analysis of Circumcision Among Two West Central
     African Tribes." African Social Research 13:187-206.

340 Lobdell, John E. 1975. "Considerations on Ritual Subincision
     Practices." Journal of Sex Research 11/1:16-24.

341 Lokko, S. D. 1978. "Ghana: The Twin Cult." Drama Review 22:89-90.

342 MacCormack. C. P. 1977. "Biological Events and Cultural Control." Signs 3/1:93-100.

343 McKnight, D. 1973. "Sexual Symbolism of Food Among the Wik-Mungkan." Man 8/2:194-209.

344 Meigs, A. S. 1976. "Male Pregnancy and the Reduction of Sexual Opposition in a New Guinea Highlands Society." Ethnology 15:393-407.

345 Mernissi, Fatima. 1977. "Women, Saints, and Sanctuaries." Signs 3/1:101-12.

346 Munroe, R. L., and R. H. Munroe. 1973. "Psychological Interpretation of Male Initiation Rites: The Case of Male Pregnancy Symptoms." Ethos 1/4:490-98.

347 Needham, Rodney. 1962. Structure and Sentiment. Chicago: University of Chicago Press.

348 Neusner, J. 1970. "Phenomenon of the Rabbi in Late Antiquity: The Ritual of Being a Rabbi in Later Sasanian Babylonia." Numen 17:1-18.

349 Paige, K. E. 1977. "Sexual Pollution: Reproductive Sex Taboos in American Society." Journal of Social Issues 33/2:144-65.

350 Paige, Karen Erickson, and Jeffrey M. Paige. 1981. The Politics of Reproductive Ritual. Berkeley: University of California Press.

351 Pernet, Henry. 1982. "Masks and Women: Toward a Reappraisal." History of Religions 22/1:45-59.

352 Poirer, Richard. 1971. The Performing Self: Compositions and Decomposition in the Languages of Contemporary Life. New York: Oxford University Press.

353 Polhemus, Ted, ed. 1978. Social Aspects of the Human Body. Harmondsworth, Eng.: Penguin.

354 Rapoport, A. 1979. "God and Zaddik as the Two Focal Points of Hasidic Worship." History of Religions 18:296-325.

355 Rappaport, Roy A. 1980. "Concluding Comments on Ritual and Reflexivity." Semiotica 30/1-2:182-93.

356 Reminick, R. A. 1976. "The Symbolic Significance of Ceremonial Defloration Among the Amhara of Ethiopia." American
Ethnologist 3/4:751-63.

357 Scheff, T. J. 1977. "Distancing of Emotion in Ritual." Current Anthropology 18:483-505.

358 Siegmann, W., and J. Perani. 1976. "Men's Masquerades of
Sierra Leone and Liberia." African Arts 9:42-7.

359 Singer, Philip, and Daniel Edward Desole. 1967. "The Australian Subincision Ceremony Reconsidered: Vaginal Envy or
Kangaroo Bifid Penis Envy." American Anthropologist 69/3:
355-7.

360 Skultans, Vieda. 1970. "The Symbolic Significance of Men-
struation and the Menopause." Man (N.S.) 5:638-51.

361 Smith-Rosenberg, Carroll. 1975. "The Female World of Love
and Ritual: Relations Between Women in Nineteenth Century
America." Signs: Journal of Women in Culture and Society
1/1:1-29.

362 Spicker, Stuart F., ed. 1970. The Philosophy of the Body:
Rejections of Cartesian Dualism. Chicago: Quadrangle Books.

363 Todd, Mabel E. 1968. The Thinking Body. New York:
Dance Horizons.

364 Vlahos, Olivia. 1979. Body, the Ultimate Symbol: Meanings
of the Human Body Through Time and Space. New York:
Lippincott.

365 Vogel, Arthur. 1973. Body Theology: God's Presence in
Man's World. New York: Harper & Row.

366 Wayman, Alex. 1982. "The Human Body as Microcosm in
India, Greek Cosmology and Sixteenth Century Europe."
History of Religions 22/2:172-90.

367 Whitten, Norman E., Jr. 1974. "Ritual Enactment of Sex
Roles in the Pacific Lowlands of Ecuador-Colombia." Ethnology 13/2:129-43.

368 Williamson, M. H. 1979. "Cicatrization of Women Among the
Kwoma." Mankind 12/1:35-41.

369 Zelman, E. C. 1977. "Reproduction, Ritual and Power."
American Ethnologist 4/4:714-33.

1.8 DIVINE BEINGS
(Gods, Demons, Spirits, Animals,
Saints, Ancestors)

370 Brown, Peter. 1981. The Cult of the Saints: Its Rise and
     Function in Latin Christianity. Chicago: University of
     Chicago Press.

371 Burl, Aubrey. 1981. Rites of the Gods. London: Dent.

372 Freed, Ruth S., and Stanley A. Freed. 1962. "Two Mother
     Goddess Ceremonies of Delhi State in the Great and Little
     Traditions." Southwestern Journal of Anthropology 18/3:
     246-77.

373 Hall, R. L. 1976. "Ghosts, Water Barriers, Corn and Sacred
     Enclosures in the Eastern Woodlands." American Antiquity
     41:360-4.

374 Hawley, J. S. and Donna Wulff, eds. 1982. The Divine Con-
     sort. Berkeley: University of California Press.

375 Kinsley, David R. 1979. The Divine Player: A Study of
     Krsna Lila. Livingston, NJ: Orient Book Distributors.

376 Kooij, K. R. van. 1972. Worship of the Goddess According
     to the Kalikapurana. Leiden: Brill.

377 Lodrick, Deryck O. 1981. Sacred Cows, Sacred Places:
     Origins and Survivals of Animal Homes in India. Berkeley:
     University of California Press.

378 Margul, Tadeusz. 1968. "Present-Day Worship of the Cow
     in India." Numen 15:63-80.

379 Patai, Raphael. 1967. The Hebrew Goddess. New York:
     Ktav.

380 Preston, James, ed. 1982. Mother Worship: Themes and
     Variations. Chapel Hill: University of North Carolina Press.

381 Robertson, Noel. 1982. "The Ritual Background of the Dying
     God in Cyprus and Syro-Palestine." Harvard Theological
     Review 75/3:313-59.

382 Shull, E. M. 1968. "Worship of the Tiger-God and Religious
     Rituals Associated with Tigers Among the Dangi Hill Tribes
     of the Dangs District Gujarat State Western India." Eastern
     Anthropologist 21/2:201-7.

383 Singer, Milton, ed. 1966. Krishna: Myths, Rites and Attitudes. Chicago: University of Chicago Press.

384 Starhawk. 1979. The Spiral Dance: Rebirth of the Ancient Religion of the Goddess. New York: Harper & Row.

385 Vogt, Evon Zartman. 1976. Tortillas for the Gods: A Symbolic Analysis of Zinacantecan Rituals. Cambridge, MA: Harvard University Press.

386 Warner, Maria. 1976. Alone of All Her Sex: The Myth and Cult of the Virgin Mary. New York: Alfred Knopf.

387 Willis, Roy. 1974. Man and Beast. Frogmore, Eng.: Paladin.

388 Wolf, E. R. 1958. "The Virgin of Guadelupe: Mexican National Symbol." Journal of American Folklore 71:34-9.

1.9 LANGUAGE
(Sound, Song, Poetry, Word, Story, Myth)

389 Abrahams, R. D., and R. Bauman. 1971. "Sense and Nonsense in St. Vincent: Speech Behavior and Decorum." African Anthropologist 73/3:762-72.

390 Ahern, Emily M. 1979. "The Problem of Efficacy: Strong and Weak Illocutionary Acts." Man 14/1:1-17.

391 Bauman, Richard. 1975. "Verbal Art as Performance." American Anthropologist 77/2:290-311.

392 Coward, Harold. 1982. "The Meaning and Power of Mantras." Studies in Religion 11/4:365-75.

393 Dane, J. A. 1978. "Aesthetics of Myth in the Redentin Easterplay." Germanic Review 53:89-95.

394 Dauenhauer, B. P. 1975. "Some Aspects of Language and Time in Ritual Worship." International Journal for Philosophy of Religion 6:54-62.

395 Davenport, W. 1975. "Lyric Verse and Ritual in the Santa Cruz Islands." Expedition 18/1:39-47.

396 Donakowski, Conrad L. 1977. A Muse for the Masses: Ritual and Music in an Age of Democratic Revolution 1770-1870. Chicago: University of Chicago Press.

397 Drewal, H. J. 1974. "Efe: Voiced Power and Pageantry."
     African Arts 7/2:26-9.

398 Dundes, A. 1976. "Psychoanalytic Study of the Bullroarer."
     Man 11:220-38.

399 Fenn, Richard K. 1982. Liturgies and Trials: The Seculari-
     zation of Religious Language. New York: Pilgrim.

400 Ferro-Luzzi, Gabriella Eichinger. 1977. "Ritual as Language:
     The Case of South Indian Food Offerings." Current Anthro-
     pology 18/3:507-14.

401 Finnegan, Ruth. 1969. "How to Do Things with Words:
     Performative Utterances Among the Limba of Sierra Leone."
     Man (N.S.) 4:537-52.

402 Georges, Robert. 1969. "Toward an Understanding of Story-
     telling Events." Journal of American Folklore 82:313-28.

403 Gill, Sam. 1981. Sacred Words: A Study of Navajo Religion
     and Prayer. Westport, CT: Greenwood.

404 Gonda, J. 1980. The Mantras of the Agnyupasthana and the
     Sautramani. Amsterdam: North-Holland Pub.

405 Grainger, Roger. 1974. The Language of the Rite. London:
     Darton.

406 Gray, Bennison. 1972. "Repetition in Oral Literature."
     Journal of American Folklore 84/331-4:289-303.

407 Halliday, M. A. K. 1976. "Anti-Languages." American An-
     thropologist 78/3:570-84.

408 Hutch, Richard. 1980. "The Personal Ritual of Glossolalia."
     Journal for the Scientific Study of Religion 19/3:255-66.

409 Jackson, Anthony. 1968. "Sound and Ritual." Man (N.S.)
     3/2:293-99.

410 Jason, Heda. 1969. "A Multidimensional Approach to Oral
     Literature." Current Anthropology 10:413-26.

411 Johnston, T. 1974. "Secret Initiation Songs of the Shangana-
     Tsonga Circumcision Rite: A Textual and Musical Analysis."
     Journal of American Folklore 87:328-39.

412 Kavanagh, Aidan. 1982. Elements of Rite: A Handbook of
     Liturgical Style. New York: Pueblo.

413 Keifer, R. A. 1972. "Ritual Makers and Poverty of Proclamation." Worship 46:66-76.

414 Lawson, Thomas E. 1976. "Ritual as Language." Religion 6:123-39.

415 Levi-Strauss, Claude. 1981. "Structuralism and Myth." The Kenyon Riview (N.S.) 3/2:64-88.

416 Lord, Albert B. 1960. The Singer of Tales. New York: Atheneum.

417 Needham, Rodney. 1967. "Percussion and Transition." Man (N.S.) 2:606-14.

418 _____. 1972. Belief, Language, and Experience. Chicago: University of Chicago Press.

419 Neusner, J. 1970. "Judaic Myth in Liturgy and Life." Journal of Religion 50:58-68.

420 O'Doherty, F. 1973. "Ritual as a Second-Order Language." Paper prepared for Burg-Watenstein Conf. 59 on Ritual and Reconciliation.

421 Ong, Walter. 1967. The Presence of the Word: Some Prolegomena for Cultural and Religious History. New Haven, CT: Yale University Press.

422 _____. 1977(a). "African Drums and Oral Noetics." New Literary History 8/3:411-29.

423 _____. 1977(b). "Marantha: Death and Life in the Text of the Book." Journal of the American Academy of Religion 45/4:419-49.

424 Patterson, Daniel W. 1979. The Shaker Spiritual. Princeton, NJ: Princeton University Press.

425 Pitt-Rivers, Julian. 1967. "Words and Deeds: The Ladinos of Chiapas." Man (N.S.) 2:71-86.

426 Powell, Jon T., and D. Dry. 1977. "Communication Without Commitment." Journal of Communication 27/3:118-21.

427 Ray, Benjamin. 1973. "'Performative Utterances' in African Rituals." History of Religions 13/1:16-35.

428 Rayfield, J. R. 1972. "What Is a Story?" American Anthropologist 74:1085-1106.

429 Ricoeur, Paul. 1973. "The Model of the Text: Meaningful
     Action Considered as a Text." New Literary History 5/1:
     91-117.

430 Saliers, Don E. 1978. "Language in the Liturgy." Worship
     52:482-575.

431 _____. 1980. The Soul in Paraphrase: Prayer and the
     Religious Affections. New York: Seabury.

432 Scheub, Harold. 1977. "Body and Image in Oral Narrative
     Performance." New Literary History 8/3:345-67.

433 Searle, John. 1969. Speech Acts. Cambridge, Eng.:
     Cambridge University Press.

434 Stahl, A. 1979. "Ritualistic Reading Among Jews." Anthro-
     pological Quarterly 52/2:115-20.

435 Sturtevant, William C. 1968. "Categories, Percussion and
     Physiology." Man (N.S.) 3:133-34.

436 Tambiah, S. J. 1968. "The Magical Power of Words."
     Man (N.S.) 3/2:175-208.

437 Tedlock, Dennis. 1977. "Toward an Oral Poetics." New
     Literary History 8/3:507-19.

438 Wagner, Roy. 1978. Lethal Speech: Daribi Myth as Sym-
     bolic Obviation. Ithaca, NY: Cornell University Press.

439 Ware, James H., Jr. 1981. Not with Words of Wisdom: Per-
     formative Language and Liturgy. Washington, DC: Univer-
     sity Press of America.

440 Wheelock, Wade. 1980. "A Taxonomy of the Mantras in the
     New- and Full-Moon Sacrifice." History of Religions 19/4:349-
     69.

441 _____. 1982. "The Problem of Ritual Language: From In-
     formation to Situation." Journal of the American Academy of
     Religion 50/1:49-71.

442 Younger, Paul. 1982. "Singing the Tamil Hymnbook in the
     Tradition of Ramanuja: The Adyayanotsva Festival in
     Srirankam." History of Religions 20/3:272-93.

1.10 QUALITY, QUANTITY, THEME

443 Beck, Brenda. 1969. "Colour and Heat in South Indian Ritual." Man (N.S.) 4:553-72.

444 Gill, S. D. 1975. "Color in Navajo Ritual Symbolism: An Evaluation of Methods." Journal of Anthropological Research 31:350-63.

445 Gonda, J. 1974. "Triads in Vedic Ritual." Ohio Journal of Religious Studies 2:5-23.

446 Gowdra, Gurumurthy K. 1971. "Ritual Circles in a Mysore Village." Sociological Bulletin 20/1:24-38.

447 Stivers, Richard. 1982. Evil in Modern Myth and Ritual. Athens: University of Georgia Press.

PART 2. RITUAL TYPES

2.1 RITES OF PASSAGE
(Couvade, Birth, Baptism, Initiation,
Puberty, Circumcision)

448 Bhattacharyya, N. N. 1968. Indian Puberty Rites. Calcutta:
Vedams.

449 Brain, J. L. 1977. "Sex, Incest, and Death: Initiation Rites
Reconsidered." Current Anthropology 18:191-208.

450 Breidenbach, Paul S. 1978. "Ritual Interrogation and the
Communication of Belief in a West African Religious Movement." Journal of Religion in Africa 9/2:95-108.

451 Brown, Judith K. 1963. "A Cross-Cultural Study of Female
Initiation Rites." American Anthropologist 65/4:837-53.

452 Brown, K. I. 1972. "Forms of Baptism in the African Inde-
pendent Churches of Tropical Africa." Practical Anthropology 19:169-82.

453 Cafferata, John. 1975. Rites. New York: McGraw-Hill.

454 Calinescu, M. 1979. "Between History and Paradise: Initiation Trials." Journal of Religion 59:218-23.

455 Campbell, Joseph. 1973. "The Importance of Rites," in his
Myths to Live By. New York: Viking.

456 Cherry, J. F. 1974. "Baptismal Rites in an Early Christian
Basilica at Stobi, Macedonia." The Baptist Quarterly 25:350-
53.

457 Clark, L. H. 1976. "Girls' Puberty Ceremony of the San Car-
los Apaches." Journal of Popular Culture 10:431-48.

458 Crawford, Marion P. 1973. "Retirement: A Rite de Passage."
Sociological Review 21/3:447-61.

459 Downing, J. 1962. "Reflections on Christian Initiation."
     Studia Liturgica 1:254-62.

460 Driver, Harold E. 1969. "Girls' Puberty Rites and Matrilocal
     Residence." American Anthropologist 71/5:905-08.

461 Eberly, Charles G. 1967. "The Influence of the Fraternity
     Ritual." College Student Survey 1/1:9-10,14.

462 Eggan, Fred, and William Henry Scott. 1963. "Ritual Life
     of the Igorots of Saganda: From Birth to Adolescence."
     Ethnology 2/1:40-54.

463 Eliade, Mircea. 1965. Rites and Symbols of Initiation. New
     York: Harper & Row.

464 _____. 1967. "Australian Religions: Initiation Rites and
     Secret Cults." History of Religions 7:61-90.

465 _____. 1969. "Initiation and the Modern World," in his
     The Quest. Chicago: University of Chicago Press.

466 Erling, B. 1973. "Rites of Christian Initiation." The Lutheran
     Quarterly 25:254-69.

467 Frederick, J. B. M. 1973. "Initiation Crisis in the Church of
     England." Studia Liturgica 9/3:137-57.

468 Fueter, P. D. 1964. "African Contribution to Christian Edu-
     cation." Practical Anthropology 11:1-13.

469 Gallen, John, ed. 1976. Made, Not Born: New Perspectives
     on Christian Initiation and the Catechumenate. Notre Dame,
     IN: University of Notre Dame Press.

470 George, A. R. 1972. "Christian Initiation." Journal of Ec-
     clesiastical History 23:65-8.

471 Girardot, N. J. 1979. "Initiation and Meaning in the Tale of
     Snow White and the Seven Dwarves." Journal of American
     Folklore 90:274-300.

472 Glaser, Barney, and Anselm L. Strauss. 1971. Status Pas-
     sage. Chicago: Atherton.

473 Glenday, David K. 1980. "Acholi Birth Ceremonies and In-
     fant Baptism: A Pastoral Paper." Missiology 8:167-76.

474 Granzberg, G. 1972. "Hopi Initiation Rites: A Case Study
     of the Validity of the Freudian Theory of Culture." Journal
     of Social Psychology 87/2:189-95.

475 _____. 1973. "The Psychological Integration of Culture:
     A Cross-Cultural Study of Hopi Type Initiation Rites."
     Journal of Social Psychology 90/1:3-7.

476 Gray, D. 1978. "Revival of the Law: The Probable Spread
     of Initiation Circumcision to the Coast of Western Australia."
     Oceania 48:188-201.

477 Greenfield, R. C. 1974. "Trial by Fire: Rites of Passage
     into Psychotherapy Groups." Perspectives in Psychiatric
     Care 12/4:152-56.

478 Guerrette, R. H. 1969. "New Rite of Infant Baptism."
     Worship 43:224-30.

479 Herdt, Gilbert H., ed. 1982. Rituals of Manhood: Male
     Initiation in Papua New Guinea. Berkeley: University of
     California Press.

480 Heron, J. 1962. "Christian Initiation." Studia Liturgica
     1:31-46.

481 Herzog, John D. 1973. "Initiation and High School in the
     Development of Kikuiju Youth's Self-Concept." Ethos 1/4:
     478-89.

482 Hinchliff, P. B. 1963. "Revising Christian Initiation Rites:
     Practical Problems in South Africa." Studia Liturgica
     2:273-83.

483 Holloman, R. E. 1974. "Ritual Opening and Individual Trans-
     formation: Rites of Passage at Esalen." American Anthro-
     pologist 76:265-80.

484 Jagger, P. J. 1971. "Anglican Rite of Infant Baptism: A
     Decade of Revision." Worship 45:22-36.

485 Kaelber, W. O. 1978. "Dramatic Element in Brahmanic Initia-
     tion: Symbols of Death, Danger, and Difficult Passage."
     History of Religions 18:54-76.

486 Kapenzi, Geoffry Z. 1975. "Rites of Passage in Four African
     Tribes." Missiology 3:65-70.

487 Kavanaugh, A. 1972. "Initiation, Baptism and Confirmation:
     Phenomonology of Christian Initiation." Worship 46:262-76.

488 _____. 1974(a). "Christian Initiation of Adults: The
     Rites." Worship 48:318-35.

489 _____. 1974(b). "New Roman Rites of Adult Initiation."
     Studia Liturgica 10/1:35-47.

490 _____. 1974(c). "Norm of Baptism: The New Rite of Christian Initiation of Adults." Worship 48:143-52.

491 _____. 1978. The Shape of Baptism: The Rites of Christian Initiation. New York: Pueblo.

492 Keifer, R. A. 1974. "Christian Initiation: The State of the Question." Worship 48:392-404.

493 Kett, Joseph F. 1977. Rites of Passage: Adolescence in America, 1790 to Present. New York: Basic Books.

494 Kloos, Peter. 1969. "Female Initiation Among the Maroni River Caribs." American Anthropologist 71/5:898-905.

495 Kretschmar, Georg. 1977. "Recent Research on Christian Initiation." Studia Liturgica 12/2-3:87-106.

496 Kupferer, Harriet J. K. 1965. "Couvade: Ritual or Real Illness." American Anthropologist 67/1:99-101.

497 Leemon, Thomas A. 1972. The Rites of Passage in a Student Culture. New York: Teacher's College.

498 Lincoln, Bruce. 1981. Emerging from the Chrysalis: Studies in Rituals of Women's Initiation. Cambridge, MA: Harvard University Press.

499 McCarl, R. S., Jr. 1976. "Smokejumper Initiation: Ritualized Communication in a Modern Occupation." Journal of American Folklore 89:49-66.

500 Mercurio, Joseph. 1974. "Caning: Educational Ritual." Australian and New Zealand Journal of Sociology 10/1:49-53.

501 Mitchell, L. L. 1961. "Baptismal Rite in Chrysostom." Anglican Theological Review 43:397-403.

502 _____. 1962. "Ambrosian Baptismal Rites." Studia Liturgica 1:24-53.

503 _____. 1966. Baptismal Anointing. London: SPCK.

504 Mitchell, N. 1974. "Christian Initiation: Decline and Dismemberment." Worship 48:458-79.

505 Moreton, M. J. 1971. "Groundwork for Initiation." Theology 74:522-29.

506 Muuss, Rolf E. 1970. "Puberty Rites in Primitive and Modern Societies." Adolescence 5/17:109-28.

507 Newing, E. G. 1970. "Baptism of Polygamous Families:
     Theory and Practice in an East-African Church." Journal
     of Religion in Africa 3/2:130-41.

508 Norbeck, Edward, et al. 1962. "The Interpretation of Data:
     Puberty Rites." American Anthropologist 64/3:463-85.

509 Ohel, M. Y. 1973. "The Circumcision Ceremony Among Im-
     migrants from Tripolitania in the Israeli Village of Dalton."
     Israel Annals of Psychiatry and Related Disciplines 11/1:
     66-71.

510 Olson, Wayne C. 1979. "Ceremony as Religious Education."
     Religious Education 74:563-69.

511 Parker, S., et al. 1975. "Father Absence and Cross-Sex
     Identity: The Puberty Rites Controversy Revisited."
     American Ethnologist 2/4:687-706.

512 Paul, Lois, and Benjamin D. Paul. 1975(a). "The Maya Mid-
     wife as Sacred Specialist: A Guatemalan Case." American
     Ethnologist 2/4:707-26.

513 _____. 1975(b). "Recruitment to a Ritual Role: The Mid-
     wife in a Maya Community." Ethos 3/3:449-67.

514 Pollock, G. H. 1973. "Jewish Circumcision: A Birth and
     Initiation Rite of Passage." Israel Annals of Psychiatry and
     Related Disciplines 11/4:297-300.

515 Ramzy, Ishak, and Keith Bryant. 1962. "Notes on Initiation
     and Hazing Practices." Psychiatry 25/4:354-62.

516 Rank, Gustav. 1962. "The Symbolic Bow in the Birth Rites
     of North Eurasian Peoples." History of Religions 1:281-90.

517 Rigby, Peter. 1967. "The Structural Context of Girls' Pu-
     berty Rites." Man 2/3:434-44.

518 Rivere, P. G. 1974. "The Couvade: A Problem Reborn."
     Man 9/3:423-35.

519 Roberts, William O., Jr. 1982. Initiation to Adulthood: An
     Ancient Rite of Passage in Contemporary Form. New York:
     Pilgrim.

520 Schlegel, A., and H. Barry. 1979. "Adolescent Initiation
     Ceremonies: A Cross-Cultural Code." Ethnology 18/2:
     199-210.

521 Schwartz, Gary, and Don Merten. 1968. "Social Identity

and Expressive Symbols: The Meaning of an Initiation Ritual." American Anthropologist 70/6:1117-31.

522 Scully, V. 1972. "In Praise of Women: The Mescalero Puberty Ceremony." Art in America 60:70-7.

523 Sofue, Takao. 1965. "Childhood Ceremonies in Japan: Regional and Local Variations." Ethnology 4/2:148-64.

524 Stookey, Laurence. 1977. "Three New Initiation Rites." Worship 51:33-49.

525 Strathern, Andrew. 1970. "Male Initiation in New Guinea Highlands Societies." Ethnology 9/4:373-79.

526 Tripp, David. 1977. "Initiation Rites of the Cathari." Studia Liturgica 12/4:184-94.

527 Turner, C. V. 1964. "Socio-Religious Significance of Baptism in Sinasina." Practical Anthropology 11:179-80.

528 Van Gennep, Arnold. 1960. The Rites of Passage. Trans. Monika B. Vizedom and Gabrielle L. Caffee. Chicago: University of Chicago Press.

529 Wainwright, G. 1969. Christian Initiation. Richmond, VA: John Knox Press.

530 _____. 1974. "Rites and Ceremonies of Christian Initiation: Developments in the Past." Studia Liturgica 10/1: 2-24.

531 Waldhorn, Arthur, and Hilda Waldhorn, eds. 1966. The Rite of Becoming: Stories and Studies of Adolescence. New York: New American Library.

532 Weiss, Charles. 1962. "A Worldwide Survey of the Current Practice of Milah (Ritual Circumcision)." Jewish Social Studies 24/1:30-48.

533 Weiss, S., and P. H. Weiss. 1976. "A Public School Ritual Ceremony." Journal of Research and Development in Education 9/4:22-8.

534 Wells, M. H. 1978. "Rites of Passage: What Makes a Ceremony?" Humanist 38:34-5.

535 Westerhoff, John H. 1979. "Joining the Church or Witnessing to Faith: Initiatory Rites Within Protestant Churches." Character Potential: A Record of Research 9/1:23-31.

536 Whitaker, E. C. 1972. "Christian Initiation." Theology
     75:424-25.

537 Willoughby, Harold R. 1960. Pagan Regeneration: A Study
     of Mystery Initiations in the Graeco-Roman World. Chicago:
     University of Chicago Press.

538 Young, Frank W. 1962. "The Function of Male Initiation
     Ceremonies: A Cross-Cultural Test of an Alternative Hy-
     pothesis." American Journal of Sociology 67/4:379-96.

539 _____. 1965. Initiation Ceremonies: A Cross-Cultural
     Study of Status Dramatization. Indianapolis: Bobbs-
     Merrill.

2.2 MARRIAGE RITES

540 Apte, Usham. 1978. The Sacrament of Marriage in Hindu
     Society from Vedic Period to Dharmasastras. Delhi: Ajanta.

541 Aries, P. 1976. "Rituals of Marriage." Canadian Journal of
     History 11:88-93.

542 Babaeva, R. 1967. "Materials for the Study of Marriage
     Ceremonies on the Apsheron Penninsula in the Past."
     Soviet Anthropology and Archaeology 6/2:3-11.

543 Barth, F. H. 1978. "Marriage Traditions and Customs Among
     Transylvanian Saxons." Eastern European Quarterly 12:93-
     110.

544 Berger, Peter, and Hansfried Kellner. 1964. "Marriage and
     the Construction of Reality." Biogenes 46:1-24.

545 Bloch, M. 1978. "Marriage Amongst Equals: An Analysis of
     the Marriage Ceremony of the Merina of Madagascar." Man
     13:21-33.

546 Cavanero, B. G. 1974. "Tribal Marriage (Philippines)."
     Contemporary Review 224:101-04.

547 Chatterjee, Chanchal Kumar. 1978. Studies in the Rites and
     Rituals of Hindu Marriage in Ancient India. Calcutta:
     Sanskrit Pustak Bhandar.

548 Coote, R. B. 1972. "Serpent and Sacred Marriage in North-
     west Semitic Tradition." Harvard Theological Review 65:
     594-95.

549 Eggan, Fred, and William Henry Scott. 1965. "Ritual Life on the Igorots of Sagada: Courtship and Marriage." Ethnology 4/1:77-112.

550 Hara, M. 1974. "Note on the Raksasa Form of Marriage." American Oriental Society Journal 94:296-306.

551 Hertsens, Luc. 1976. "Family Life and Marriage Among Christians in Sub-Saharan Africa." Pro Mundi Vita African Dossier 2:1-62.

552 Kitahara, M. 1974. "A Function of Marriage Ceremony." Anthropologica 16/2:163-75.

553 Lejeune, Michel. 1980. "Towards a Ritual of Marriage: Sacrament of Life." African Ecclesial Review 22:151-58.

554 Mason, J. P. 1975. "Sex and Symbol in the Treatment of Women: The Wedding Rite in a Libyan Oasis Community." American Ethnologist 2/4:649-61.

555 Metzger, Duane, and Gerald E. Williams. 1963. "A Formal Ethnographic Analysis of Tenejapa Ladino Weddings." American Anthropologist 65/5:1076-1101.

556 Monger, G. 1973. "Pre-Marriage Ceremonies (Great Britain)." Journal of American Folklore 86:391-92.

557 Norman, Sam R. 1979. "Ceremony for the Divorced." Journal of Pastoral Care 33:60-3.

558 Oracion, Timoteo S. 1964. "Magahat Marriage Practices." Philippine Sociological Review 15/1-2:101-09.

559 Parker, S. B. 1976. "Marriage Blessing in Israelite and Ugaritic Literature." Journal of Biblical Literature 95:23-30.

560 Patel, H. L. 1973. "Reference Group Behaviour of a Khatriya Caste in a Western Indian Village." Society and Culture 4/1:1-10.

561 Sloyan, G. S. 1970. "New Rite for Celebrating Marriage." Worship 44:258-70.

562 Stevenson, Kenneth. 1983. Nuptial Blessing: A Study of Christian Marriage Rites. New York: Oxford University Press.

563 Strange, H. 1976. "Continuity and Change: Patterns of Mate Selection and Marriage Ritual in a Malay Village." Journal of Marriage and the Family 38:561-71.

564 Strobel, M. 1975. "Women's Wedding Celebration." African
     Studies Review 18:35-45.

565 Tsong-Yuan, Lin. 1965. "Marriage Rites Among the Taromak
     Rukai and the Chala?abus Paiwan." Bulletin of the Depart-
     ment of Archaeology and Anthropology 25-26:145-56.

566 Vetscher, Trande. 1973. "Betrothal and Marriage Among the
     Minas of South Rajasthan." Man in India 53/4:387-413.

567 Weir, Shelagh, and Widad Kawar. 1975. "Costumes and Wed-
     ding Customs in Bayt Dajan." Palestine Exploration Quarterly
     107:39-51.

568 Wimberley, Howard. 1969. "Self-Realization and the Ancestors:
     An Analysis of Two Japanese Ritual Procedures for Achieving
     Domestic Harmony." Anthropological Quarterly 42/1:37-51.

2.3 FUNERARY RITES
(Mortuary Rites, Death, Mourning,
Unction, Burial, Cremation)

569 Ablon, Joan. 1970. "The Samoan Funeral in Urban America."
     Ethnology 9/3:209-27.

570 Aries, P. 1974(a). "Death Inside Out: Eight Centuries of
     Death in the West." The Hastings Center Report 2/2:3-18.

571 _____. 1974(b). Western Attitudes Toward Death. Balti-
     more: Johns Hopkins Press.

572 Bond, P. B. 1967. "Celebration of Death." Architectural
     Review 141:303-04.

573 Bryer, K. B. 1979. "The Amish Way of Death: A Study of
     Family Support Systems." American Psychologist 34/3:
     255-61.

574 Bynum, J. 1973. "Social Status and Rites of Passage: The
     Social Context of Death." Omega: Journal of Death and Dy-
     ing 4/4:323-32.

575 Carter, William E. 1968. "Secular Reinforcement in Aymara
     Death Ritual." American Anthropologist 70/2:238-63.

576 Chesterman, J. T. 1977. "Burial Rites in a Cotswold Long
     Barrow." Man 12:22-32.

577 Chow, L. 1964. "Problem of Funeral Rites." Practical Anthropology 11:226-28.

578 Concepcion, Mercedes B. 1962(a). "Ritual Mourning: A
Cross-Cultural Comparison." Philippine Sociological Review
10/3-4:182-86.

579 _____. 1962(b). "Ritual Mourning: Culturally Specified
Crowd Behaviour." Anthropological Quarterly 35/1:1-9.

580 Couveinhes, D. 1974. "Maya Burial Customs." Diogenes
88:100-13.

581 Danforth, Loring M. 1982. The Death Rituals of Rural
Greece. Princeton, NJ: Princeton University Press.

582 Deegan, M. J. 1975. "The Symbolic Passage from the Living
to the Dead for the Visibly Injured." International Journal
of Symbology 6/3:1-14.

583 Faron, Louis C. 1963. "Death and Fertility Rites of the
Mapuche (Araucanian) Indians of Central Chile." Ethnology
2/2:135-56.

584 Finnestad, B. Bjerre. 1978. "The Meaning and Purpose of
Opening the Mouth in Mortuary Contexts." Numen 25:118-34.

585 Fiske, A. M. 1969. "Death: Myth and Ritual." Journal of
the American Academy of Religion 37:249-65.

586 Gerson, G. S. 1977. "The Psychology of Grief and Mourning
in Judaism." Journal of Religion and Health 16/4:260-74.

587 Goldschmidt, W. 1973. "Guilt and Pollution in Sebei Mortuary
Rituals." Ethos 1/1:75-105.

588 Goody, Jack. 1962. Death, Property and the Ancestors.
Stanford, CA: Stanford University Press.

589 Gray, D. 1976. "Aboriginal Mortuary Practices in Carnarvon."
Oceania 47:144-56.

590 Hertz, Robert. 1960. Death and the Right Hand. Trans. R.
& C. Needham. Glencoe, IL: Free Press.

591 Hoon, Paul W. 1976. "Theology, Death, and the Funeral
Liturgy." Union Seminary Quarterly Review 31:169-81.

592 Huff, V. E., and K. M. Dimick. 1969. "Death Rites: An
Alternative Approach." Pastoral Psychology 20:35-8.

593 Huntington, Richard, and Peter Metcalf. 1979. Celebrations
     of Death: The Anthropology of Mortuary Ritual. Cambridge,
     Eng.: Cambridge University Press.

594 Jernigan, H. L. 1973. "Some Reflections on Chinese Patterns
     of Grief and Mourning." Southeast Asia Journal of Theology
     15/1:21-47.

595 Jha, Makhan. 1966. "Death-Rites Among Maithil Brahmans."
     Man in India 46/3:241-47.

596 Kinsley, David. 1975. "Freedom from Death in the Worship
     of Kali." Numen 22:183-207.

597 Kjaerum, P. 1967. "Mortuary Houses and Funeral Rites in
     Denmark." Antiquity 41:190-96.

598 Kyriakakis, James. 1974. "Byzantine Burial Customs: Care
     of the Deceased from Death to the Prothesis." The Greek
     Orthodox Theological Review 19:37-72.

599 Lindig, Wolfgang H. 1964. "Tree Burial Among the Seri
     Indians." Ethnology 3/3:284-86.

600 Lippy, C. H. 1977. "Sympathy Cards and Death." Theology
     Today 34:167-77.

601 McCombie, F. 1978. "At His Heels a Stone." Notes and
     Queries 25:139-41.

602 Mathias, E. 1974. "Italian-American Funeral: Persistence
     Through Change." Western Folklore 33:35-50.

603 Meyers, E. M. 1971. "Theological Implications of an Ancient
     Jewish Burial Custom." The Jewish Quarterly Review 62:
     95-119.

604 Moser, M. J. 1975. "Death in Chinese: A Two-Dimensional
     Analysis." Journal of Thanatology 3/3:169-85.

605 Mosse, G. 1979. "National Cemeteries and National Revival:
     The Cult of the Fallen Soldiers in Germany." Journal of
     Contemporary History 14:1-20.

606 Palgi, Phyllis. 1975. "Death of a Soldier: Sociocultural Ex-
     pressions." Adolescent Psychiatry 4:174-98.

607 Paolini, J. 1969. "Kabyle Handling of Grief, Kabyle Popular
     Islam: Background to the Burial Rites." Muslim World
     59:251-74.

608   Pine, V. R. 1969. "Comparative Funeral Practices." Practi-
      cal Anthropology 16:49-62.

609   Plath, David W. 1964. "Where the Family of God ... Is the
      Family: The Rite of the Dead in Japanese Households."
      American Anthropologist 66/2:300-17.

610   Rowell, G. 1977. The Liturgy of Christian Burial. London:
      SPCK.

611   Rutherford, R. 1980. The Death of a Christian: The Rite
      of Funerals. New York: Pueblo.

612   Saraswati, Baidyanath. 1967. "The Tadakhi Custom of Cre-
      mation." Man in India 47/4:263-71.

613   Stannard, David E. 1977. The Puritan Way of Death: A
      Study in Religion, Culture, and Social Change. New York:
      Oxford University Press.

614   Steele, Richard L. 1977. "Dying, Death, and Bereavement
      Among the Maya Indians of Mesoamerica: A Study in An-
      thropological Psychology." American Psychologist 32/12:
      1060-68.

615   Swift Arrow, B. 1974. "Funeral Rites of the Quechan Tribe."
      Indian Historian 7:22-4.

616   Van den Berghe, P. L. 1978. "El Cargo de las Animas:
      Mortuary Rituals and the Cargo System in Highland Peru."
      Anthropological Quarterly 51:129-36.

617   Whitaker, E. C. 1961. "Unction in the Syrian Baptismal
      Rite." Church Quarterly Review 162:176-87.

618   Wilke, P. J. 1978. "Cairn Burials of the California Deserts."
      American Antiquity 43:444-48.

619   Wolowelsky, J. B. 1974. "Midrash on Jewish Mourning."
      Judaism 23:212-15.

620   Wright, G. R. H. 1969. "Strabo on Funerary Customs at
      Petra." Palestine Exploration Quarterly 101:113-16.

2.4 FESTIVALS
(Celebrations, Feasts, Carnivals,
Contests, Sports, Games)

621 Adlard, John. 1972. The Sports of Cruelty. London:
     Cecil and Amelia Woolf.

622 Andreasen, N. E. 1974. "Festival and Freedom: A Study
     of an Old Testament Theme." Interpretation 28:281-97.

623 Arnold, I. R. 1972. "Festivals of Ephesus." American Jour-
     nal of Archaeology 76:17-22.

624 Azouf, Mona. 1975. "Space and Time in the Festivals of the
     French Revolution." Comparative Studies in Society and
     History 17/3:372-84.

625 Babb, Lawrence A. 1975. "Walking on Flowers in Singapore:
     A Hindu Festival Cycle." Ekistics 39:332-38.

626 Bell, R. H. 1978. "Understanding the Fire-Festivals: Witt-
     genstein and Theories in Religion." Religious Studies 14:
     113-24.

627 Blauvelt, M., and J. P. C. Floyd. 1976. "Shape of Celebra-
     tion." Architectural Record 160:81-6.

628 Bouissac, Paul. 1976. Circus and Culture: A Semiotic Ap-
     proach. Bloomington: Indiana University Press.

629 Browning, Robert L. 1980. "Festivity: From a Protestant
     Perspective." Religious Education 75/3:273-81.

630 Chase, R. A. 1977. "Fairs and Festivals." Man-Environment
     Systems 7/3:117-44.

631 Cherniack-Tzuriel, A. 1977. "Omer Festival of Kibbutz
     Ramat Yochanan." Drama Review 21:11-20.

632 _____. 1978. "Festivals and Folkcultures." Scandinavian
     Review 66:75-9.

633 Cheska, A. T. 1979. "Sports Spectacular: A Ritual Model
     of Power." International Review of Sport Sociology 14/2:
     51-72.

634 Clothey, F. W. 1969. "Skanda-Sasti: A Festival in Tamil
     India." History of Religions 8:236-59.

635 Gavrielides, Nicolas. 1974. "Name Days and Feasting: Social

and Ecological Implications of Visiting Patterns in a Greek Village of the Argolid." Anthropological Quarterly 47/1: 48-70.

636 Gilbert, W. S. 1975. "International Festivals '75: Shiraz-Presepolis." Plays and Players 23:15-17.

637 Gilmore, D. 1975. "Carnival in Fuenmayor: Class Conflict and Social Cohesion in an Andalusian Town." Journal of Anthropological Research 31/4:331-49.

638 Goodger, John. 1982. "Judo Players as a Gnostic Sect." Religion 12:333-44.

639 Griessman, B. E. 1976. "Tukabatchi Pow Wow and the Spirit of Tecumseh: Or, How to Hold a Pow Wow Without Indians." Phylon 37:172-73.

640 Grimes, Ronald L. 1976. Symbol and Conquest: Public Ritual and Drama in Santa Fe, New Mexico. Ithaca, NY: Cornell University Press.

641 Gulati, R. K. 1968. "Pongal: A Deeply Tradition-Oriented Festival of the Deep South." Journal of Social Research 11/2:150-54.

642 Guttman, Allen. 1978. From Ritual to Record: The Nature of Modern Sports. New York: Columbia University Press.

643 Hennelly, Mark M. 1977-78. "Games and Ritual in 'Deliverance.'" Journal of Altered States of Consciousness 3/4: 337-53.

644 Hutchison, A. 1975. "Argungu Fishing Festival." Africa Report 20:47-9.

645 Isambert, F. A. 1969. "Feasts and Celebrations: Some Critical Reflections on the Idea of Celebration." Trans. Bernd Jager. Humanitas 5:29-42.

646 James, Erwin O. 1961. Seasonal Feasts and Festivals. New York: Barnes and Noble.

647 Kearny, M. 1969. "An Exception to the 'Image of Limited Good.'" American Anthropologist 71/5:888-90.

648 Kohara, Y. 1973. "Folk Without Festivals." The Japan Interpreter 8/1:55-62.

649 Kojiro, Y., and K. Matsumoto. 1975. "Six Japanese Village Festivals." Ekistics 39:339-56.

650 McPhee, P. 1978. "Popular Culture, Symbolism and Rural
     Radicalism in Nineteenth-Century France." The Journal of
     Peasant Studies 5/2:238-53.

651 Mangin, William. 1961. "Fiestas in an Indian Community in
     Peru." Ed. Viola E. Garfield. Proceedings of the 1961 An-
     nual Spring Meeting of the American Ethnological Society.

652 Manning, F. E. 1978. "Carnival in Antigua (Caribbean Sea):
     An Indigenous Festival in a Tourist Economy." Anthropos
     73/1-2:191-204.

653 _____. 1981. "Celebrating Cricket: The Symbolic Con-
     struction of Caribbean Politics." American Ethnologist 8/3:
     616-32.

654 _____. 1983. The Celebration of Society: Perspectives on
     Contemporary Cultural Performance. London, Ont.: Congress
     of Social and Humanistic Studies.

655 Martin, Gerhard M. 1976. Fest: The Transformation of
     Everyday. Trans. M. Douglas Meeks. Philadelphia: For-
     tress.

656 Melia, D. F. 1978. "Grande Tromenie at Locronan: A Major
     Breton Lughnasa Celebration." Journal of American Folklore
     91:528-42.

657 Metraux, G. S., ed. 1976. Cultures, vol. 3. Paris: Unesco
     Press.

658 Morgenstern, J. 1964. "Festival of Jereboam I." Journal of
     Biblical Literature 83:109-18.

659 Myers, Robert. 1972. Celebrations: The Complete Book of
     American Holidays. Garden City, NY: Doubleday.

660 Newall, V. 1974. "Allendale Fire Festival in Relation to Its
     Contemporary Social Setting." Folklore 85:93-103.

661 Novak, Michael. 1976. The Joy of Sports: End Zones,
     Bases, Baskets, Balls and the Consecration of the American
     Spirit. New York: Basic Books.

662 Parke, H. W. 1977. Festivals of the Athenians. Ithaca, NY:
     Cornell University Press.

663 Pignatti, T. 1975. "Venetian Festivals and Amusements."
     Apollo 102:208-15.

664 Ploeg, A. 1973. "Feasting for Gain and Help." Mankind
     9:15-24.

Festivals (2.4) 83

665 Rearick, C. 1977. "Festivals in Modern France: The Experience of the Third Republic." Journal of Contemporary History 12:435-60.

666 Renwick Gallery. 1982. Celebration: A World of Art and Ritual. Washington, DC: Smithsonian.

667 Rheubottom, D. B. 1976. "Saint's Feast and Skopska Crna Goran Social Structure." Man 11:18-34.

668 Riegelhaupt, J. F. 1975. "Festas and Padres: The Organization of Religious Action in a Portuguese Parish." Ekistics 39:324-31.

669 Samuelson, Sue. 1982. Christmas: An Annotated Bibliography of Analytical Scholarship. New York: Garland.

670 Sandall, R. 1978. "Way to the Pig Festival." Encounter 51:63-70.

671 Stanley, J. M. 1977. "Special Time, Special Power: The Fluidity of Power in a Popular Hindu Festival." Journal of Asian Studies 37:27-43.

672 Stewart, R. A. 1971. "Jewish Festivals." The Evangelical Quarterly 43:149-61.

673 Tenfelde, K. 1978. "Mining Festivals in the Nineteenth Century." Journal of Contemporary History 13:377-412.

674 Tortosa, J. M. 1972. "Ritual and Cultural Lag: The Feast of San Isidro in Tiraque." Social Compass 19/4:613-16.

675 Turner, Victor, ed. 1982(a). Celebration: Studies in Festivity and Ritual. Washington, DC: Smithsonian.

676 _____. 1982(b). From Ritual to Theater: The Human Seriousness of Play. New York: Performing Arts.

677 Von Grunebaum, G. E. 1981. Muhammadam Festivals: Typical Elements of Islamic Rituals, Prayers and Pilgrimage. New York: State Mutual Book.

678 Wunder, R. P. 1967. "Forgotten French Festival in Rome." Apollo 85:354-59.

2.5 PILGRIMAGE
(Quests, Processions, Parades)

679 Bhardwaj, Surinder Mohan. 1973. Hindu Places of Pilgrimage
     in India. Berkeley: University of California Press.

680 Davies, Horton and Marie-Helene. 1982. Holy Days and Holi-
     days: The Mediaeval Pilgrimage to Compostela. Lewisburg,
     PA: Bucknell University Press.

681 Gross, Daniel R. 1971. "Ritual and Conformity: A Religious
     Pilgrimage to Northeastern Brazil." Ethnology 10/2:129-48.

682 Hawley, John S., and Shrivatsa Goswami. 1981. At Play with
     Krishna: Pilgrimage Dramas from Brindavan. Princeton,
     NJ: Princeton University Press.

683 Holmes, Urban T. 1973. "Revivals are Un-American: A Re-
     calling of America to Its Pilgrimage." Anglican Theological
     Review 1:58-75.

684 Kamal, Ahmad. 1961. The Sacred Journey: Being Pilgrimage
     to Makkah. New York: Duell, Sloan and Pearce.

685 Turner, V. W. 1973. "Center Out There: Pilgrim's Goal."
     History of Religions 12:191-230.

686 _____, and Edith Turner. 1978. Image and Pilgrimage in
     Christian Culture: Anthropological Perspectives. New York:
     Columbia University Press.

687 Turner, Victor. 1979. Process, Pilgrimage and Performance:
     A Study in Comparative Symbology. New Delhi: Concept.

2.6 PURIFICATION
(Fasts, Pollution, Taboo, Sin, Confession)

688 Achte, Kalle A. 1975. "Use of Water as a Mode of Psychiatric
     Treatment." Psychiatria Fennica n.v.:93-100.

689 Anant, Victor. 1976. "A Woman's Own World." New Society
     35/691:12-14.

690 Awolalu, J. O. 1976. "Sin and Its Removal in African Tra-
     ditional Religion." Journal of the American Academy of Re-
     ligion 44:275-87.

691 Bettelheim, Bruno. 1962. Symbolic Wounds. New York:
     Collier.

692 Blau, J. L. 1967. "Red Heifer: A Biblical Purification Rite
     in Rabbinic Literature." Numen 14:70-8.

693 Buchanan, G. W. 1963. "Role of Purity in the Structure of
     the Essene Sect." Revue de Qumran 4:397-406.

694 Bumgarten, J. M. 1967. "Essene Avoidance of Oil and the
     Laws of Purity." Revue de Qumran 6:183-92.

695 Carroll, M. P. 1978. "One More Time: Leviticus Revisited."
     European Journal of Sociology 19/2:339-46.

696 Cohen, P. T. 1974. "Paeng Baan: The Purification and Re-
     generation of a Village in Northern Thailand." Mankind
     9:319-23.

697 Douglas, Mary. 1978. Purity and Danger: An Analysis of
     Concepts of Pollution and Taboo. Boston: Routledge and
     Kegan Paul.

698 Dyer, R. R. 1969. "Evidence for Apolline Purification Rit-
     uals at Delphi and Athens." Journal of Hellenic Studies
     89:38-56.

699 Elkins, R. 1964. "Anit Taboo: A Manobo Cultural Unit."
     Practical Anthropology 11:185-88.

700 Ferro-Luzzi, Gabriella Eichinger. 1974. "Women's Pollution
     Periods in Tamiland." Anthropos 69/1-2:113-61.

701 Fishbane, Michael. 1974. "Accusations of Adultery: A Study
     of Law and Scribal Practice in Numbers 5:11-31." Hebrew
     Union College Annual 45:25-45.

702 Fuller, C. J. 1976. "Kerala Christians and the Caste Sys-
     tem." Man 11:53-70.

703 Hershman, P. 1974. "Hair, Sex and Dirt." Man 9/2:274-98.

704 Hoenig, S. B. 1969. "Qumran Rules of Impurities." Revue
     de Qumran 6:559-67.

705 Khare, R. S. 1962. "Ritual Purity and Pollution in Relation
     to Domestic Sanitation." Eastern Anthropologist 15/2:125-39.

706 Mahar, Pauling Moller. 1960. "A Ritual Pollution Scale for
     Ranking Hindu Castes." Sociometry 23/3:293-306.

707 Meigs, A. S. 1978. "Papuan Perspective on Pollution." Man
     13:304-18.

708 Neufeld, E. 1971. "Purification, Ritual and Hygiene." Bibli-
     cal Archaeologist 34:63-6.

709 Neusner, Jacob. 1975. "Idea of Purity in Ancient Judaism."
     Journal of the American Academy of Religion 43:15-26.

710 Rosen, Leora Nadine. 1973. "Contagion and Cataclysm: A
     Theoretical Approach to the Study of Ritual Pollution Be-
     liefs." African Studies 32/4:229-46.

711 Salamone, Frank A. 1975. "Continuity of Igbo Values After
     Conversion: A Study in Purity and Prestige." Missiology
     3:33-43.

712 Saraf, Samarendra. 1969. "The Hindu Ritual Purity-Pollution
     Complex." Eastern Anthropologist 22/2:161-76.

713 Singh, T. R. 1966. "Some Aspects of Ritual Purity and Pol-
     lution." Eastern Anthropologist 19/2:131-43.

2.7 CIVIL CEREMONY
(Royal Rites, Enthronement,
Legal Ceremony, Warfare)

714 Anglo, S. 1969. Spectacle, Pageantry and Early Tudor Policy.
     New York: Oxford University Press.

715 Appadurai, Arjun. 1978. Rituals of the Kandyan State.
     London: Cambridge University Press.

716 Arno, A. 1976. "A Ritual of Reconciliation and Village Con-
     flict Management in Fiji." Oceania 47:49-65.

717 Beidelman, T. O. 1966. "Swazi Royal Ritual." Africa 36:
     373-405.

718 Bellah, Robert. 1974. "Civil Religion in America," in
     American Civil Religion. Ed. Russell E. Richey and Donald
     G. Jones. New York: Harper & Row.

719 _____. 1975. The Broken Covenant: American Civil Re-
     ligion in Time of Trial. New York: Seabury.

720 Bergeron, D. M. 1970. "Venetian State Papers and English
     Civic Pageantry, 1558-1642." Renaissance Quarterly 23/1:
     37-47.

721 Binnis, Christopher. 1982. "Soviet Secular Ritual: Atheist Propaganda or Spiritual Consumerism?" Religion in Communist Lands. 10/3:298-309.

722 Bocock, Robert J. 1970. "Ritual: Civic and Religious." British Journal of Sociology 21:285-97.

723 Bowden, R. 1979. "Tapu and Mana: Ritual Authority and Political Power in Traditional Maori Society." Journal of Pacific History 14/1-2:50-61.

724 Capps, D. 1979. "Erikson's Theory of Religious Ritual: The Case of the Excommunication of Ann Hibbens." Journal for the Scientific Study of Religion 18:337-49.

725 Carr, G. Lloyd. 1979. "Is the Song of Songs a 'Sacred Marriage' Drama?" Journal of the Evangelical Theological Society 22:103-14.

726 Cohen, Abner. 1971. "The Politics of Ritual Secrecy." Man (N.S.) 6:427-49.

727 Dillon, R. G. 1976. "Ritual Resolution in Meta' Legal Process." Ethnology 15:287-99.

728 Donahue, Bernard I. 1975. "The Political Use of Religious Symbols: A Case Study of the 1972 Presidential Campaign." Review of Politics 37/1:48-65.

729 Edelman, Murray. 1969. "Calation and Ritualization of Political Conflict." American Behavioral Scientist 13/2:231-46.

730 Ellwood, Robert S. 1973. The Feast of Kingship: Accession Ceremonies in Ancient Japan. Tokyo: Sophia.

731 Endleman, Robert. 1967. "The Military as a Rite de Passage." In his Personality and Social Life. New York: Random House.

732 Freed, Ruth S., and Stanley A. Freed. 1966. "Unity in Diversity in the Celebration of Cattle-Curing Rites in a North Indian Village: A Study in the Resolution of Conflict." American Anthropologist 68/3:673-92.

733 Gluckman, Max. 1965. Politics, Law and Ritual in Tribal Society. Chicago: Aldine.

734 Goodin, R. E. 1978. "Rites of Rulers." British Journal of Sociology 29:281-99.

735 Hiltebeitel, Alf. 1975. The Ritual of Battle: Krishna in the Mahabharata. Ithaca, NY: Cornell University Press.

736 Hovda, Robert W. 1980. "The Vesting of Liturgical Ministers."
     Worship 54:98-117.

737 Jaspard, J. M. 1972. "Ritual Law and Structuration in the
     Child's Religious Attitude." Social Compass 19/3:459-71.

738 Kantorowicz, E. H. 1958. Laudes Regiae: A Study in Litur-
     gical Acclamations and Medieval Ruler Worship. Berkeley:
     University of California Press.

739 Kertzer, D. I. 1974. "Politics and Ritual: The Communist
     Festa in Italy." Anthropological Quarterly 47:374-89.

740 Koch, K. F., et al. 1977. "Ritual Reconciliation and the
     Obviation of Grievances: A Comparative Study in the
     Ethnography of Law." Ethnology 16:269-84.

741 Koenker, Ernest B. 1965. Secular Salvations: The Rites and
     Symbols of Political Religions. Philadelphia: Fortress.

742 La Fontaine, J. 1977. "Power of Rights." Man 12:421-37.

743 Lane, C. 1979. "Ritual and Ceremony in Contemporary Soviet
     Society." Sociological Review (N.S.) 27:253-78.

744 Lipsitz, Lewis. 1968. "If, as Verba Says, 'the State Func-
     tions as Religion,' What Are We to Do Then to Save Our
     Souls?" American Political Science Review 62/2:527-35.

745 Lor, Aaron. 1975. "From Civil to Traditional Religion."
     Religious Education 70:514-18.

746 Lukes, Steven. 1975. "Political Ritual and Social Integration."
     Sociology 9/2:289-308.

747 MacCormack, Sabine G. 1981. Art and Ceremony in Late
     Antiquity. Berkeley: University of California Press.

748 McDowell, Jennifer. 1974. "Soviet Civil Ceremonies." Jour-
     nal for the Scientific Study of Religion 13/3:265-79.

749 Manning, Frank. 1980. "Go Down, Moses: Revivalist Politics
     in a Caribbean Mini-State," in Political Anthropology Year
     Book I. Ed. Myron J. Aronoff. New Brunswick, NJ:
     Transaction.

750 _____. 1983. "Carnival and the West Indian Diaspora."
     The Round Table 286:186-96.

751 Middlekauff, Robert. 1970. "The Ritualization of the American
     Revolution," in The Development of an American Culture.

Ed. Stanley Cohen and Lorman Ratner. Englewood Cliffs, NJ: Prentice-Hall.

752 Moulierac, H. 1977. "Strike: War or Festival." Diogenes 98:55-70.

753 Muir, E. 1979. "Images of Power: Art and Pageantry in Renaissance Venice." American History Review 84:16-52.

754 Neiburg, H. L. 1970. "Agonistics: Rituals of Conflict." The Annals of the American Academy of Political and Social Science 391:56-73.

755 Neusner, Jacob. 1975. "Ritual Without Myth: The Use of Legal Materials for the Study of Religions." Religion 5:91-100.

756 Richey, Russell E., and Donald Y. Jones, eds. 1974. American Civil Religion. New York: Harper & Row.

757 Scullard, H. H. 1981. Festivals and Ceremonies of the Roman Republic. Ithaca, NY: Cornell University Press.

758 Seneviratne, H. L. 1977. "Politics and Pageantry: Universalisation of Ritual in Sri Lanka." Man 12:65-75.

759 Strong, Roy. 1973. Splendour at Court: Renaissance Spectacle and the Theatre of Power. Boston: Houghton Mifflin.

760 Trout, A. 1977. "Louis XIV's Paris: Government and Ceremony." History Today 27:14-21.

761 Warner, William Lloyd. 1962. American Life: Dream and Reality. Chicago: University of Chicago Press.

762 Wilson, John F. 1979. Public Religion in American Culture. Philadelphia: Temple University Press.

2.8 RITUALS OF EXCHANGE
(Hunting, Agricultural Rites, Ritual Ecology,
Meals, Food Offerings, Potlatch)

763 Barker, G. 1976. "Ritual Estate and Aboriginal Polity." Mankind 10/4:225-39.

764 Blackman, M. B. 1977. "Bracelets and Boas: The Potlatch in Photographs." Anthropological Papers of the University of Alaska 18/2:53-67.

765 Bodewitz, H. W. 1976. The Daily Evening and Morning Of-
     fering (Agnihotra) According to the Brahmanas. Leiden:
     Brill.

766 Bolton, R. 1979. "Guinea Pigs, Protein, and Ritual."
     Ethnology 18:229-52.

767 Cancian, F. 1974. "New Patterns of Stratification in the
     Zinacantan Cargo System." Journal of Anthropological Re-
     search 30:164-73.

768 Chinodya, S. 1976. "Rainmaking in Zimbabwe." Africa Re-
     port 21:47-50.

769 Cole, Arthur H. 1962. "The Price System and Rites of
     Passage." American Quarterly 14:4.

770 Cooper, Eugene. 1982. "The Potlatch in Ancient China."
     History of Religions 22/2:103-28.

771 Ellwood, R. S. 1968. "Harvest and Renewal at the Grand
     Shrine of Ise." Numen 15:165-90.

772 Gregory, J. R. 1975. "Image of Limited Good, or Expecta-
     tion of Reciprocity?" Current Anthropology 16:73-92.

773 Heinen, H. D., and K. Ruddle. 1974. "Ecology, Ritual, and
     Economic Organization in the Distribution of Palm Starch
     Among the Warao of the Orinoco Delta." Journal of Anthro-
     pological Research 30/2:116-38.

774 Hippler, A. E., et al. 1975. "The Psychocultural Significance
     of the Alaska Athabascan Potlatch Ceremony." Psychoanalytic
     Study of Society 6:204-34.

775 Kottak, Conrad P. 1978. "Rituals at McDonalds." Journal of
     American Culture 1/2:370-76.

776 Landa Jocano, Felipe. 1967. "Agricultural Rituals in a
     Philippine Barrio." Philippine Sociological Review 15/1-2:
     48-55.

777 Lincoln, Bruce. 1981. Priests, Warriors, and Cattle: A Study
     in the Ecology of Religions. Berkeley: University of California
     Press.

778 Madigan, Francis Cunningham, S. J. 1964. "The Harvest Rit-
     ual in North Central Mindano." Sociological Analysis 25/4:
     231-37.

779 Opler, Morris E. 1968. "Remuneration to Supernaturals and
     Man in Apachean Ceremonialism." Ethnology 7/4:356-93.

780 Price, Richard. 1966. "Fishing Rites and Recipes in a Mar-
     tiquan Village." Caribbean Studies 6/1:3-24.

781 Pulsford, R. L. 1975. "Ceremonial Fishing for Tuna by the
     Motu of Pari." Oceania 46:107-13.

782 Rappaport, Roy A. 1967. "Ritual Regulation of Environmental
     Relations Among a New Guinea People." Ethnology 6/1:17-30.

783 _____. 1968. Pigs for Ancestors: Ritual in the Ecology of
     a New Guinea People. New Haven, CT: Yale University
     Press.

784 Robolos, Zenaida M. 1964. "Promissory and Debt Aspects of
     the Folk Ritual in Misamis Oriental." Philippine Sociological
     Review 12/1-2:95-101.

785 Rutz, H. J. 1978. "Ceremonial Exchange and Economic De-
     velopment in Village Fiji." Economic Development and Cul-
     tural Change 26:777-805.

786 Tiffany, S. W. 1975. "Giving and Receiving: Participation
     in Chiefly Redistribution Activities in Samoa." Ethnology
     14/3:267-86.

787 Tiffany, S. W., and W. W. Tiffany. 1978. "Optation, Cog-
     natic Descent and Redistributions in Samoa." Ethnology
     17:367-90.

788 Walker, A. R. 1978. "Lahu Nyi (Red Lahu) Farming Rites."
     Anthropos 73/5-6:717-36.

789 Wasserstom, R. 1978. "Exchange of Saints in Zinacantan:
     The Socioeconomic Bases of Religious Change in Southern
     Mexico." Ethnology 17:197-210.

790 Whitten, N. E., Jr. 1978. "Ecological Imagery and Cultural
     Adaptability: The Canelos Quichua of Eastern Ecuador."
     American Anthropologist 80:836-59.

791 Wolowelsky, Joel B. 1977. "Human Meal." Judaism 26:92-6.

792 Yalman, N. 1973. "On the Meaning of Food Offerings in
     Ceylon." Social Compass 20/2:287-302.

2.9 SACRIFICE
(Decapitation, Cannibalism, Executions,
Violence, Atonement)

793 Aguilar, H. 1976. The Sacrifice in the Rgveda: Doctoral
     Aspects. Delhi: Bharatiya Vidya Prakashan.

794 Awolalu, J. O. 1973. "Yoruba Sacrificial Practice." Journal
     of Religion in Africa 5/2:81-93.

795 Beidelman, T. O. 1969. "Ox and Nuer Sacrifice." Man
     4:290-91.

796 Beit-Hallahmi, B. 1976. "Sacrifice, Fire and the Victory of
     the Sun: A Search for the Origins of Hanukkah." Psycho-
     analytic Review 63/4:497-509.

797 Bourdillon, M. F. C., and Meyer Fortes. 1980. Sacrifice.
     London: Academic Press.

798 Collins, John J. 1977. "Meaning of Sacrifice: A Contrast of
     Methods." Biblical Research 22:19-34.

799 Converse, H. S. 1974. "Agnicayana Rite: Indigenous Ori-
     gin?" History of Religions 14:81-95.

800 Daly, Robert. 1978(a). Christian Sacrifice: The Judaeo-
     Christian Background Before Origen. Washington, DC:
     Catholic University of America Press.

801 _____. 1978(b). The Origins of the Christian Doctrine of
     Sacrifice. Philadelphia: Fortress.

802 Deshen, Shlomo. 1979. "The Kol Nidre Enigma: An Anthro-
     pological View of the Day of Atonement Liturgy." Ethnology
     18/2:121-33.

803 Drury, Naama. 1981. The Sacrificial Ritual in the Satapatha
     Brahmana. Delhi: Motilal Banarsidass.

804 Earhart, H. B. 1966. "Ishikozume: Ritual Execution in Jap-
     anese Religion, Especially in Shugendo." Numen 13:116-27.

805 Foucault, Michel. 1978. "The Spectacle of the Scaffold."
     Ch. 2 of his Discipline and Punish: The Birth of the Prison.
     Trans. Alan Sheridan. New York: Random House.

806 Gill, D. 1974. "Trapezomata: A Neglected Aspect of Greek
     Sacrifice." Harvard Theological Review 67:117-37.

807 Girard, René. 1977. Violence and the Sacred. Trans.
     Patrick Gregory. Baltimore: Johns Hopkins University
     Press.

808 Gray, G. B. 1971. Sacrifice in the Old Testament: Its
     Theory and Practice. New York: Ktav.

809 Hecht, Richard. 1982. "Studies on Sacrifice." Religious
     Studies Review 8/3:253-59.

810 Hubert, Henri, and Marcel Mauss. 1964. Sacrifice: Its Na-
     ture and Function. Trans. W. D. Halls. Chicago: University
     of Chicago Press.

811 James, E. O. 1962. Sacrifice and Sacrament. London:
     Thames & Hudson.

812 McCarthy, D. J. 1969. "Symbolism of Blood and Sacrifice."
     Journal of Biblical Literature 88:166-76.

813 Moser, C. L. 1974. "Ritual Decapitation in Moche Art."
     Archaeology 27:30-7.

814 Neusner, J. 1979. "Map Without Territory: Mishnah's Sys-
     tem of Sacrifice and Sanctuary." History of Religions 19:
     103-27.

815 Niles, J. D. 1977. "Lamkin: The Motivation of Horror."
     Journal of American Folklore 90:49-67.

816 Omoyajowo, J. A. 1973. "Human Destiny, Personal Rites and
     Sacrifices in African Traditional Religion." Journal of Reli-
     gious Thought 30/1:5-15.

817 Ortiz de Montellano, B. R. 1978. "Aztec Cannibalism: An
     Ecological Necessity?" Science 200/4342:611-17.

818 Prince, R. 1975. "Symbols and Psychotherapy: The Exam-
     ple of Yoruba Sacrificial Ritual." Journal of the American
     Academy of Psychoanalysis 3/3:321-38.

819 Rainey, A. F. 1970. "Order of Sacrifices in Old Testament
     Ritual Texts." Biblica 51/4:485-98.

820 Sagan, Eli. 1974. Cannibalism: Human Aggression and Cul-
     tural Form. New York: Harper & Row.

821 Schlesinger, K. 1976. "Origins of the Passover Seder in
     Ritual Sacrifice." Psychoanalytic Study of Society 7:369-99.

822 Shulman, D. 1978. "Serpent and the Sacrifice: An Anthill
     Myth from Tiruvarur." History of Religions 18:107-37.

823   Smith. J. Oates.   1966.   "Ritual and Violence in Flannery
      O'Connor."   Thought   41/163:545-59.

824   Smith, M.   1975.   "Note on Burning Babies."   American Orien-
      tal Society Journal   95:477-79.

825   Thite, Ganesh Umakant.   1970.   "Animal-Sacrifice in the
      Brahmana Texts."   Numen   17:143-58.

826   Thompson, S. I.   1975.   "Torture and Execution of Surrogate
      Kinsmen in Two Societies: The Ainu and the Tupinamba."
      Journal of Social Psychology   95:19-26.

827   Turner, Victor.   1977.   "Sacrifice as Quintessential Process:
      Prophylaxis or Abandonment?"   History of Religions   16:189-
      215.

828   Van Baaren, T. P.   1964.   "Theoretical Speculations on Sacri-
      fice."   Numen   11:1-12.

829   Willey, G. R.   1976.   "Mesoamerican Civilization and the Idea
      of Transcendence."   Antiquity   50:205-15.

2.10   WORSHIP
(Liturgy, Prayer, Sacraments)

830   Adams, Doug.   1975.   Involving the People in Dancing Worship:
      Historic and Contemporary Patterns.   Austin, TX: Sharing Co.

831   Adams, Doug, and Judith Rock.   1979.   Biblical Criteria in
      Modern Dance: Modern Dance as a Prophetic Form.   Austin,
      TX: Sharing Co.

832   Andronikof, C.   1976.   "The Meaning of Rite."   St. Vladimir's
      Theological Quarterly   20/1-2:3-8.

833   Baer, R. A., Jr.   1974.   "Moods and Modes of Worship."
      Theology Today   31:220-27.

834   Bateson, Mary Catherine.   1972.   "Magic and Sacrament."
      Worship   46:98-104.

835   Bebis, G. S.   1976.   "Influence of Jewish Worship on Orthodox
      Christian Worship."   Journal of Ecumenical Studies   13:562-68.

836   Bellah, Robert.   1970.   "The Dynamics of Worship," in his
      Beyond Belief: Essays on Religion in a Post-Traditional
      World.   New York: Harper & Row.

837 Bellamak, Lu. 1978. Non-Judgmental Sacred Dance: Simple
     Ways to Pray Through Dance. Austin, TX: Sharing Co.

838 Bouyer, Louis. 1963. Rite and Man. London: Burns Oates.

839 Bro, Bernard. 1968. "Man and the Sacraments: The An-
     thropological Substructure of the Christian Sacraments."
     Concilium 31:33-50.

840 Buchanan, George W. 1980. "Worship, Feasts and Ceremonies
     in the Early Jewish-Christian Church." New Testament
     Studies 26:279-97.

841 Burkhart, John E. 1982. Worship. Philadelphia: Westminster.

842 Burns, T. A., and J. S. Smith. 1978. "Symbolism of Becom-
     ing in a Sunday Service of an Urban Black Holiness Church."
     Anthropological Quarterly 51:185-204.

843 Burtchaell. James T. 1971. "The Rituals of Jesus, the Anti-
     Ritualist." Journal of the American Adademy of Religion
     39/4:513-25.

844 Cipolla, R. G. 1973. "Ceremonial and the Tacit Dimension."
     Worship 47:398-404.

845 Collins, Mary. 1975. "Liturgical Methodology and the Cultural
     Evolution of Worship in the United States." Worship 49:85-
     102.

846 _____. 1979. "Critical Ritual Studies: Examining an Inter-
     section of Theology and Culture," in The Bent World: Es-
     says on Religion and Culture. Ed. John R. May. Chico,
     CA: Scholars Press.

847 Crehan, Joseph H. 1979. "The Theology of Eucharistic Con-
     secration: Role of the Priest in Celtic Liturgy." Theologi-
     cal Studies 40:334-43.

848 Damien, Muma. 1977. "Man-Centered Liturgy (Africa)."
     African Ecclesial Review 19:31-8.

849 Davies, J. G., ed. 1972. A Dictionary of Liturgy and Wor-
     ship. New York: Macmillan.

850 Davies, J. K. 1967. "Demosthenes on Liturgies: A Note."
     Journal of Hellenic Studies 87:33-40.

851 Davis, C. 1970. "Ghetto or Desert: Liturgy in a Cultural
     Dilemma." Studia Liturgica 7/2-3:10-27.

852 Davis, Horton. 1978. "Jacob's Ladder: A Study of Experiment and Tradition in Modern Christian Worship." Encounter 39:367-83.

853 De Coppens, Peter Roche. 1977. The Nature and Use of Ritual: The Great Christian Documents and Traditional Blueprints for Human and Spiritual Growth. Washington, DC: University Press of America.

854 Dixon, John W., Jr. 1976. "Liturgy as an Art Form." Anglican Theological Review (Supplementary Series) 6:55-68.

855 Eaton, John H. 1981. Vision in Worship: The Religion of Prophecy and Liturgy in the Old Testament. London: SPCK.

856 Gay, Volney P. 1978. "Public Rituals Versus Private Treatment: Psychodynamics of Prayer." Journal of Religion and Health 17/4:244-60.

857 Gill, Sam D. 1977. "Prayer as Person: The Performative Force in Navaho Prayer Acts." History of Religions 17/2: 143-57.

858 Hanning, R. W. 1973. "'You Have Begun a Parlous Playe': The Nature and Limits of Dramatic Mimesis as a Theme in Four Middle English 'Fall of Lucifer' Cycle Plays." Comparative Drama 7:22-50.

859 Hefling, Charles C. 1979. "Liturgy and Myth: A Theological Approach Based on the Methodology of Bernard Lonergan." Anglican Theological Review 61:200-23.

860 Hellwig, Monika. 1976. "Christian Eucharist in Relation to Jewish Worship." Journal of Ecumenical Studies 13:322-30.

861 Henderson, E. H. 1973. "Christian Transformation of the Ritual Way." Anglican Theological Review 55:189-200.

862 Hine, Virginia H. 1981. "Self-generated Ritual: Trend or Fad?" Worship 55:404-19.

863 Hoche-Mong, Raymond. 1976. "Artistic Dimension of Liturgy." Studia Liturgica 11/2:118-36.

864 Holmes, Urban T. 1973. "Liminality and Liturgy." Worship 47/7:386-99.

865 _____. 1977(a). "Ritual and the Social Drama." Worship 51:197-213.

866 _____. 1977(b). "What Has Manchester to Do with Jerusalem?" Anglican Theological Review 5911:79-97.

867 Idelson, A. Z. 1967. Jewish Liturgy and Its Development.
     New York: Schocken.

868 Jenson, Robert W. 1983. "The Praying Animal." Zygon
     18/3:311-25.

869 Jones, Paul D. 1974. Rediscovering Ritual. Paramus, NJ:
     Paulist Press.

870 Jordahl, L. D. 1970. "Liturgy and Ceremony: Catholic-
     Protestant Cross Currents." Worship 44:171-81.

871 Kiesling, Christopher. 1977. "Liturgy and Social Justice."
     Worship 51:351-61.

872 Lardner, Gerald V. 1979. "Evaluative Criteria and the
     Liturgy." Worship 53:357-70.

873 Laurentin, A. 1969. "Theatre and Liturgy." Trans. J. C.
     Kirby. Worship 43:382-406.

874 Lawler, Michael G. 1980. "Christian Rituals: An Essay in
     Sacramental Symbolisms." Horizons 7:7-35.

875 Lopresti, James J. 1978. "Rituals and Hopes." Worship
     52:348-58.

876 McKenna, John H. 1976. "Ritual Activity." Worship 50:
     347-52.

877 Mahoney, F. W. 1971. "Aymara Indians: A Model for Litur-
     gical Adaptation." Worship 45:405-13.

878 Martimort, A. G., ed. 1968. The Church at Prayer: Intro-
     duction to the Liturgy. 4 vols. New York: Desclee.

879 Martin, David. 1979. "Profane Habit and Sacred Usage."
     Theology 82:83-95.

880 Michael, R. Blake. 1982. "Work as Worship in Virasaiva Tra-
     dition." Journal of the American Academy of Religion 50/4:
     605-19.

881 Parrinder, Geoffrey. 1976. Worship in the World's Religions.
     Totowa, NJ: Littlefield.

882 Power, David N. 1978. "Unripe Grapes: The Critical Func-
     tion of Liturgical Theology." Worship 52:386-99.

883 _____. 1980. "Cult to Culture: The Liturgical Foundation
     of Theology." Worship 54:482-95.

884 Prell-Foldes, Riv-Ellen. 1980. "The Reinvention of Reflexivity
     in Jewish Prayer: The Self and Community in Modernity."
     Semiotica 30/1-2:73-96.

885 Rahner, Karl. 1962. The Church and the Sacraments. New
     York: Herder.

886 Ramsey, Paul. 1979. "Liturgy and Ethics." Journal of Reli-
     gious Ethics 7:139-71.

887 Rappaport, Roy A. 1976. "Liturgies and Lies." International
     Yearbook for the Sociology of Knowledge 10:75-104.

888 Regan, P. 1973. "Liturgy and the Experience of Celebration."
     Worship 47:592-600.

889 Rouillard, Philippe. 1978. "From Human Meal to Christian
     Eucharist." Worship 52:425-39.

890 St. Hilaire, G. P. 1976. "Indian Sacraments: A Sanpoil
     Model." Cross Currents 26:172-88.

891 Schauer, Blase. 1982. "Towards an Anthropology of Wor-
     ship." Listening 17/3:231-38.

892 Schillebeeckx, E. 1963. Christ, the Sacrament of Encounter
     with God. New York: Sheed & Ward.

893 Schmemann, Alexander. 1966. Introduction to Liturgical The-
     ology. London: Faith Press.

894 Scott, R. Taylor. 1980. "The Likelihood of Liturgy."
     Anglican Theological Review 62:103-20.

895 Searle, Mark. 1981. "Liturgy as Metaphor." Worship 55/2:
     98-120.

896 Seaton, Linda Kahn. 1979. Scriptural Choreography: Bibli-
     cal Dance Forms in Shaping Contemporary Worship. Austin,
     TX: Sharing Co.

897 Smart, Ninian. 1972. The Concept of Worship. New York:
     St. Martin.

898 Taylor, Margaret F. 1976. Dramatic Dance with Children in
     Education and Worship. Austin, TX: Sharing Co.

899 Sullivan, Stephen. 1964. Readings in Sacramental Theology.
     Englewood Cliffs, NJ: Prentice-Hall.

900 Trolin, Clifford. 1979. Movement in Prayer in a Hasidic Mode.
     Austin, TX: Sharing Co.

901 Trotman, D. V. 1976. "Yoruba and Orisha Worship in Trinidad and British Guiana: 1838-1870." African Studies 19: 1-17.

902 Turner, Victor. 1976. "Ritual, Tribal and Catholic." Worship 50/6:504-26.

903 Viviano, Benedict T. 1978. Study as Worship: Aboth and the New Testament. Leiden: Brill.

904 Wainwright, Geoffrey. 1977. "Christian Worship and Western Culture." Studia Liturgica 12/1:20-33.

905 _____. 1980. Doxology: The Praise of God in Worship, Doctrine, and Life: A Systematic Theology. New York: Oxford University Press.

906 Ware, James H., Jr. 1981. Not with Words of Wisdom: Performative Language and Liturgy. Landham, MD: University Press of America.

907 White, J. F. 1974. "Worship and Culture: Mirror or Beacon?" Theological Studies 35:288-301.

908 Worgul, George S. 1980. From Magic to Metaphor: A Validation of the Christian Sacraments. New York: Paulist Press.

2.11 MAGIC
(Fertility, Divination, Sorcery, Oracles)

909 Adedeji, J. A. 1970. "The Origin of the Yoruba Masque Theatre: The Use of Ifa Divination Corpus as Historical Evidence." African Notes 6:1.

910 Blythin, Islwyn. 1970. "Magic and Methodology." Numen 17:45-59.

911 Butler, E. M. 1971. Ritual Magic. Hollywood, CA: Newcastle.

912 Elliott, Robert C. 1960. The Power of Satire: Magic, Ritual, Art. Princeton, NJ: Princeton University Press.

913 Fontenrose, Joseph. 1978. The Delphic Oracle: Its Responses and Operations, with a Catalogue of Responses. Berkeley: University of California Press.

914 Gonzalez-Wippler, Migene. 1973. Santeria: Magic Cults of the Caribbean. New York: Crown.

915 Gurunmurthy, K. G. 1973. "Fertility Festivals and Unity in a
     Mysore Village." Society and Culture 4/1:111-20.

916 Hooykaas. C. 1980. Drawings of Balinese Sorcery. Leiden:
     Brill.

917 Johnston, T. F. 1974. "Communication with the Fertility God
     Via Hallucinogens in Tsongaland." Religion 4:85-95.

918 King, Francis. 1970. Ritual Magic in England: 1887 to the
     Present. Cedar Knolls, NJ: Wehman.

919 _____. 1971. Rites of Modern Occult Magic. New York:
     Macmillan.

920 Lewis-Williams, J. D. 1977. "Led by the Nose: Observations
     on the Supposed Use of Southern Sand Rock Art in Rain-
     Making Rituals." African Studies 36/2:155-59.

921 Loewe, Michael, and Carmen Blacker. 1981. Oracles and Divi-
     nation. Boulder, CO; Shambala.

922 Malinowski, Bronislaw. 1954. Magic, Science and Religion,
     and Other Essays. Garden City, NY: Doubleday.

923 Middleton, John, ed. 1967. Magic, Witchcraft and Curing.
     Garden City, NY: The Natural History Press.

924 O'Keefe, Daniel L. 1982. Stolen Lightning: The Social
     Theory of Magic. New York: Continuum.

925 Orlove, B. 1979. "Two Rituals and Three Hypotheses: An
     Examination of Solstice Divination in Southern Highland
     Peru." Anthropological Quarterly 52:86-98.

926 Skultans, Vieda. 1974. Intimacy and Ritual: A Study of
     Spiritualism, Mediums and Groups. London: Routledge and
     Kegan Paul.

927 Stein, Howard F. 1974. "Envy and the Evil Eye Among
     Slovak-Americans: An Essay in the Psychological Ontogeny
     of Belief and Ritual." Ethos 2/1:15-46.

928 Tambiah, Stanley. 1973. "Form and Meaning of Magical Acts:
     A Point of View," in Modes of Thought. Eds. R. Horton and
     R. Finnegan. London: Faber and Faber.

929 Thomas, Keith. 1971. Religion and the Decline of Magic.
     New York: Scribners.

930 Turner, Victor. 1961. Ndembu Divination: Its Symbolism

and Techniques. Manchester, Eng.: Manchester University
Press.

931 _____ . 1975. Revelation and Divination in Ndembu Ritual.
Ithaca, NY: Cornell University Press.

932 Wax, Murray, and Rosalie Wax. 1962. "The Magical World
View." Journal for the Scientific Study of Religion 1/2:
179-88.

933 Wilson, Bryan. 1978. Magic and the Millennium. Woodstock,
NY: Beekman.

934 Winkelman, Michael. 1982. "Magic: A Theoretical Reassess-
ment." Current Anthropology 23/1:37-66.

2.12 HEALING RITES
(Shamanism, Psychedelics, Exorcism, Illness,
Therapy, Dream Incubation, Possession)

935 Agar, Michael. 1977. "Into That Whole Ritual Thing: Ritual-
istic Drug Use Among Urban American Heroin Addicts," in
Drugs, Rituals, and Altered States of Consciousness. Ed.
M. Du Toit. Rotterdam: A. A. Bakema.

936 Albanese, Catherine. 1980. "The Poetics of Healing: Root
Metaphors and Rituals in Nineteenth Century America."
Soundings 63/4:381-406.

937 Aldrich, M. R. 1977. "Tantric Cannabis Use in India."
Journal of Psychedelic Drugs 9/3:227-33.

938 Bahr, Donald M., et al. 1974. Piman Shamanism and Staying
Sickness. Tucson: University of Arizona Press.

939 Bee, Robert L. 1966. "Potowatomi Peyotism: The Influence
of Traditional Patterns." Southwestern Journal of Anthropology 22/2:194-205.

940 Betz, Hans. 1980. "Fragments From a Catabasis Ritual in a
Greek Magical Papyrus." History of Religions 19:287-95.

941 Bilmes, Jacob, and Alan Howard. 1980. "Pain as a Cultural
Drama." Anthropology and Humanism Quarterly 15/2-3:10-13.

942 Buxton, Jean. 1973. Religion and Healing in Mandari. Oxford, Eng.: Clarendon.

943   Cava, Ralph della. 1970. Miracle at Joaseiro. New York:
      Columbia University Press.

944   Collins, John James. 1968. "A Descriptive Introduction to
      the Taos Peyote Ceremony." Ethnology 7/4:427-49.

945   De Rios, M. D., and D. E. Smith. 1976. "Using or Abusing?
      An Anthropological Approach to the Study of Psychoactive
      Drugs." Journal of Psychedelic Drugs 8:263-66.

946   _____. 1977(a). "Drug Use and Abuse in Cross Cultural
      Perspective." Human Organization 36:14-21.

947   _____. 1977(b). "Function of Drug Rituals in Human
      Society: Continuities and Changes." Journal of Psychedelic
      Drugs 9:269-75.

948   _____. 1977(c). "Hallucinogenic Ritual as Theatre."
      Journal of Psychedelic Drugs 9:265-68.

949   Devisch, R. 1977. "Processes for the Articulation of Mean-
      ing and Ritual Healing Among the Northern Yaka (Zaire)."
      Anthropos 72/5-6:683-708.

950   Dobkin, Marlene. 1968-69. "Folk Curing with a Psychedelic
      Cactus in the North Coast of Peru." International Journal
      of Social Psychiatry 15/1:23-56.

951   Douglas, Mary. 1970. "The Healing Rite." Man (N.S.)
      5:302-08.

952   Eliade, Mircea. 1964. Shamanism: Archaic Techniques of
      Ecstasy. Trans. Willard R. Trask. Princeton, NJ: Princeton
      University Press.

953   Emboden, William. 1977. "Dionysus as a Shaman and Wine as
      a Magical Drug." Journal of Psychedelic Drugs 9/3:187-92.

954   Fischer, B. 1974. "Baptismal Exorcism in the Catholic Bap-
      tismal Rites After Vatican II." Studia Liturgica 10/1:48-55.

955   Fox, J. R. 1960. "Therapeutic Rituals and Social Structure
      in Cochiti Pueblo." Human Relations 13/4:291-304.

956   Furst, Peter T., ed. 1972. Flesh of the Gods: The Ritual
      Use of Hallucinogens. New York: Praeger.

957   Gordon, B. 1978. "Sri Lanka: The Ritual Exorcism of
      Devils." Drama Review 22:81.

958   Grossinger, Richard. 1980. Plant Medicine: From Stone-Age

Shamanism to Post-Industrial Healing. Garden City, NY:
Doubleday.

959 Gusmer, Charles W. 1972. "Liturgical Traditions of Christian
Illness: Rites of the Sick." Worship 46:528-43.

960 Halifax, Joan. 1982. Shaman: The Wounded Healer. New
York: Crossroad.

961 Halverson, J. 1971. "Dynamics of Exorcism: The Sinhalese
Ganniyakuma." History of Religions 10:334-59.

962 Harner, Michael J. 1973. Hallucinogens and Shamanism.
New York: Oxford University Press.

963 _____. 1980. The Way of the Shaman: A Guide to Power
and Healing. New York: Harper & Row.

964 Henderson, D. J. 1976. "Exorcism, Possession, and the
Dracula Cult: A Synopsis of Object-Relations Psychology."
Bulletin of the Menninger Clinic 40/6:603-28.

965 Henry, E. O. 1977. "A North Indian Healer and the Sources
of His Power." Social Science and Medicine 11/5:309-17.

966 Jilek, W. G. 1974. "Indian Healing Power: Indigenous
Therapeutic Practices in the Pacific Northwest." Psychiatric
Annals 4/11:13-21.

967 Kapferer, Bruce. 1979. "Mind, Self, and Other in Demonic
Illness: The Negation and Reconstruction of Self." American Ethnologist 6/1:110-33.

968 Katz, Richard. 1981. "Education as Transformation: Becoming a Healer Among the !Kung and the Fijians." Harvard
Educational Review 51/1:57-78.

969 Kennedy, John G. 1967. "Nubian Zar Ceremonies as Psychotherapy." Human Organization 26/4:185-94.

970 Kiev, Ari. 1964. Magic, Faith and Healing: Studies in Primitive Psychiatry Today. New York: Free Press.

971 _____. 1968. Curanderismo: Mexican-American Folk Psychiatry. New York: Free Press.

972 Koss, J. D. 1975. "Therapeutic Aspects of Puerto Rican
Cult Practices." Psychiatry 38/2:160-71.

973 Lebra, T. S. 1974. "The Interactional Perspective of Suffer-
ing and Curing in a Japanese Cult." International Journal
of Social Psychiatry 20/3-4:281-86.

974 Lee, Jung Young. 1973. "Seasonal Rituals of Korean Shaman-
     ism." History of Religions 12:271-85.

975 _____. 1974. "Communal Rituals of Korean Shamanism."
     Journal of Asian and African Studies 9:82-90.

976 _____. 1981. Korean Shamanistic Rituals. The Hague:
     Mouton.

977 Lewis, I. M. 1971. Ecstatic Religion: An Anthropological
     Study of Spirit Possession and Shamanism. Harmondsworth,
     Eng.: Penguin.

978 Loewen, J. A. 1969. "Confession, Catharsis, and Healing
     (Primitive Rites)." Practical Anthropology 16:63-74.

979 Lowenthal, I. P. 1978. "Ritual Performance and Religious
     Experience: A Service for the Gods in Southern Haiti."
     Journal of Anthropological Research 34/3:392-414.

980 McAllister, J. Gilbert. 1965. "The Four Quartz Rocks Medi-
     cine Bundle of the Kiowa-Apache." Ethnology 4/2:210-24.

981 McRae, W. E. 1975. "Peyote Rituals of the Kiowas." South-
     west Review 60:217-33.

982 Marshall, Lorna. 1969. "The Medicine Dance of the !Kung
     Bushmen." Africa 39:4.

983 Mechanic, David. 1972. "The Concept of Illness Behavior."
     Journal of Chronic Diseases 15:180-94.

984 Meigs, J. T. 1977. "Pastoral Care Methods and Demonology
     in Selected Writings." Journal of Psychology and Theology
     5/3:234-46.

985 Myerhoff, Barbara A. 1974. Peyote Hunt: The Sacred Jour-
     ney of the Huichol Indians. Ithaca, NY: Cornell University
     Press.

986 Pascarosa, P., and S. Futterman. 1976. "Ethnopsychedelic
     Therapy for Alcoholics: Observations in the Peyote Ritual
     of the Native American Church." Journal of Psychedelic
     Drugs 8:215-21.

987 Powers, William K. 1982. Yuwipi: Vision and Experience in
     Oglala Ritual. Lincoln: University of Nebraska Press.

988 Prince, R. H. 1974. "The Problem of 'Spirit Possession' as
     a Treatment for Psychiatric Disorders." Ethos 2/4:315-33.

989 Rardin, Jared J. 1979. "The Rites of Resistance: Images
     and Drama in Pastoral Psychotherapy." Journal of Pastoral
     Care 33/3:175-84.

990 Read, Margaret. 1966. Culture: Health and Disease. Lon-
     don: Tavistock.

991 Reed, Henry. 1976. "Dream Incubation: A Reconstruction
     of a Ritual in Contemporary Form." Journal of Humanistic
     Psychology 16/4:52-70.

992 Relay, M. 1977. "Ritual Madness Observed: A Discarded
     Pattern of Fate in Papua, New Guinea." Journal of Pacific
     History 12/1-2:55-79.

993 Renner, H. P. V. 1979. "The Use of Ritual in Pastoral
     Care." Journal of Pastoral Care 33:164-74.

994 Rykwert, J. 1977. "Ritual and Hysteria." Ekistics 44:296-
     300.

995 Scheff, T. J. 1979. Catharsis in Healing, Ritual, and Drama.
     Berkeley: University of California Press.

996 Schultes, R. E. 1977. "Mexico and Colombia: Two Major
     Centres of Aboriginal Use of Hallucinogens." Journal of
     Psychedelic Drugs 9:173-76.

997 Shapiro, Martin. 1978. Getting Doctored: Critical Reflec-
     tions on Becoming a Physician. Kitchener, Ont.: Between
     the Lines.

998 Siirala, Aarne. 1981. The Voice of Illness: A Study in
     Therapy and Prophecy. Toronto: Edwin Mellen Press.

999 Simonton, O. Carl. 1975. "Belief Systems and Management
     of the Emotional Aspects of Malignancy." Journal of Trans-
     personal Psychology 7/1:29-47.

1000 Steadman, Margaret. 1978. "Ritual: A Paradigm for Family
     Therapy." Dissertation Abstracts International 38/8-B:3911.

1001 Stirrat, R. L. 1977. "Demonic Possession in Roman Catholic
     Sri Lanka." Journal of Anthropological Research 33:133-57.

1002 Szasz, Thomas. 1974. Ceremonial Chemistry: The Ritual
     Persecution of Drugs, Addicts, and Pushers. Garden City,
     NY: Doubleday.

1003 Talley, Thomas J. 1972. "Healing: Sacrament or Charism."
     Worship 46/9:518-27.

1004 Wagner, R. M. 1975. "Pattern and Process in Ritual Syn-
       cretism: The Case of Peyotism Among the Navajo." Jour-
       nal of Anthropological Research 31:162-81.

1005 Waley, Arthur. 1973. The Nine Songs: A Study of Shaman-
       ism in Ancient China. San Francisco: City Lights.

1006 Wimberley, R. C., et al. 1975. "Conversion in a Billy Gra-
       ham Crusade: Spontaneous Event or Ritual Performance?"
       Sociological Quarterly 16:162-70.

2.13 INTERACTION RITES
(Ritualization, Habit, Secular Ritual)

1007 Barfield, Owen. 1979. History, Guilt and Habit. New York:
       Columbia University Press.

1008 Bateson, Mary Catherine. 1974. "Ritualization: A Study in
       Texture and Texture Change," in Religious Movements in
       Contemporary America. Ed. Zaretsky and Leone. Prince-
       ton, NJ: Princeton University Press.

1009 Burnett, Jacquetta Hill. 1969. "Ceremony, Rites and Eco-
       nomics in the Student System of an American High School."
       Human Organization 28/1:1-10.

1010 Byman, Seymour. 1978. "Ritualistic Acts and Compulsive
       Behavior: The Pattern of Tudor Martyrdom." The Ameri-
       can Historical Review 83:625-43.

1011 Chrisman, Noel J. 1974. "Middle Class Communities: The
       Fraternal Order of Badgers." Ethos 2/4:356-76.

1012 Eaton, Travis. 1969. "Religious Aspects of Freemasonry: A
       Paper in the Sociology of Religion." Proceedings of the
       Southwestern Sociological Association 19:1-5.

1013 Fischer, E. A. 1971. "Ritual as Communication." Worship
       45:73-91.

1014 Goffman, Erving. 1963(a). Behavior in Public Places. New
       York: Free Press.

1015 _____. 1963(b). Stigma: Notes on the Management of
       Spoiled Identity. Englewood Cliffs, NJ: Prentice-Hall.

1016 _____. 1967. Interaction Ritual: Essays on Face-to-Face
       Behavior. Garden City, NY; Doubleday.

1017 _____. 1971. Relations in Public: Microstudies of the
       Public Order. New York: Harper & Row.

1018 _____. 1974. Frame Analysis: An Essay on the Organi-
       zation of Experience. New York: Harper & Row.

1019 Hage, Per. 1979. "Symbolic Culinary Meditation." Man
       14/1:81-92.

1020 Heilman, Samuel C. 1976. Synagogue Life: A Study in
       Symbolic Interaction. Chicago: University of Chicago
       Press.

1021 Hockings, Paul. 1968. "On Giving Salt to Buffaloes: Ritual
       as Communication." Ethnology 7/4:411-26.

1022 Huxley, Sir Julian, et al. 1966. "A Discussion on Ritualiza-
       tion of Behavior in Animals and Man." Philosophical Trans-
       actions of the Royal Society of London. Series B, 251:247-
       526.

1023 Lorenz, Konrad. 1966. On Aggression. Trans. Marjorie
       Latzke. London: Methuen.

1024 McCarl, Robert S., Jr. 1976. "Smokejumper Initiation:
       Ritualized Communiction in a Modern Occupation."
       Journal of American Folklore 89/351:49-66.

1025 Manning, Frank. 1973. Black Clubs in Bermuda. Ithaca,
       NY: Cornell University Press.

1026 Manning, Peter. 1976. "The Decline of Civility." Canadian
       Review of Sociology and Anthropology 13/1:13-25.

1027 Mercurico, Joseph. 1974. "Caning: Educational Ritual."
       The Australian and New Zealand Journal of Sociology
       10/1:49-53.

1028 Moore, Sally Falk, and Barbara G. Myerhoff, eds. 1975.
       Symbol and Politics in Communal Ideology: Cases and
       Questions. Ithaca, NY: Cornell University Press.

1029 _____. 1977. Secular Ritual. Assen, The Netherlands:
       Van Gorcum.

1030 Myerhoff, Barbara. 1978. Number Our Days. New York:
       Simon and Schuster.

1031 Reddy, A. Munirathnam. 1973. "On the Role of Ritual
       Friendship in the Mobility of Wealth in the Visakhapatnam
       Agency." Man in India 53/3:243-55.

1032 Reyburn, W. D. 1963. "Christianity and Ritual Communica-
      tion (Among Kaka Tribesmen)." Practical Anthropology
      10:145-59.

1033 Schiffrin, D. 1977. "Opening Encounters." American Soci-
      ology Review 42:679-91.

1034 Srivastava, S. K. 1960. "Patterns of Ritual Friendship in
      Tribal India." International Journal of Comparative Soci-
      ology 1/2:239-47.

1035 Trice, Harrison M., et al. 1969. "The Role of Ceremonials
      in Organizational Behaviour." Industrial and Labor Rela-
      tions Review 23/1:40-51.

2.14 MEDITATION RITES
(Possession, Conversion, Trance)

1036 Anonymous. 1975. Mystical Rites and Rituals. London:
      Octopus.

1037 Belo, Jane. 1960. Trance in Bali. New York: Greenwood.

1038 Capwell, C. H. 1974. "Esoteric Belief of the Bauls of Ben-
      gal." Journal of Asian Studies 33:255-64.

1039 Claus, P. J. 1975. "Siri Myth and Ritual: A Mass Posses-
      sion Cult of South India." Ethnology 14:47-58.

1040 Cooper, Robert M., and W. Taylor Stevenson, eds. 1975.
      "Prayer, Ritual, and Spiritual Life: A Consultation."
      American Theological Review (Supplementary Series) No. 5.

1041 Deren, Maya. 1970. Divine Horsemen: The Voodoo Gods of
      Haiti. New York: Chelsea.

1042 Firth, Raymond. 1967. "Ritual and Drama in Malay Spirit
      Mediumship." Comparative Studies in Society and History
      9/2:190-207.

1043 Gold, P. 1977. "Stepping to the Timeless Dance: Ritual
      and the Visionary Experience." African Arts 10:68-9.

1044 Gottschall, L. D. 1974. "Western Religions and Hypnosis."
      Journal of the American Institute of Hypnosis 15/6:271-73,
      298.

1045 Greeley, Andrew M. 1970. "Superstition, Ecstasy and Tribal
      Consciousness." Social Research 37/2:203-11.

1046 Hillman, James. 1979. The Dream and the Underworld. New
       York: Harper & Row.

1047 Hitchcock, J. T. 1973. "Nepali Shaman's Performance as
       Theatre." Artscanada 30:74-80.

1048 Hutch, Richard A. 1980. "The Personal Ritual of Glosso-
       lalia." Journal for the Scientific Study of Religion 19:255-
       66.

1049 Johnson, Weldon T. 1971. "The Religious Crusade: Revival
       or Ritual?" American Journal of Sociology 76/5:873-88.

1050 Jules-Rosette, B. 1980. "Ceremonial Trance Behavior in an
       African Church: Private Experience and Public Expres-
       sion." Journal for the Scientific Study of Religion 19/1:
       1-16.

1051 Leacock, Ruth, and Seth Leacock. 1972. Spirits of the Deep:
       Drums, Mediums and Trance in a Brazilian City. Garden
       City, NY: Doubleday.

1052 Lex, Barbara W. 1975-76. "Physiological Aspects of Ritual
       Trance." Journal of Altered States of Consciousness 2/2:
       109-22.

1053 Manning, Frank. 1977. "The Salvation of a Drunk: Play
       and Reality in a Pentecostal Ritual." American Ethnologist
       4/3:397-412.

1054 Metraux, Alfred. 1972. Voodoo in Haiti. Trans. Hugo
       Charteris. New York: Schocken.

1055 Palmer, Susan. 1980. "Performance Practices in Meditation
       Rituals Among the New Religions." Studies in Religion
       9/4:403-13.

1056 Ranaghan, K. M. 1974. "Conversion and Baptism: Personal
       Experience and Ritual Celebration in Pentecostal Churches."
       Studia Liturgica 10/1:65-76.

1057 Searle, Mark. 1980. "The Journey of Conversion." Worship
       54:35-55.

2.15 RITES OF INVERSION
(Rites of Rebellion, Clowning, Joking,
Obscenity, Revitalization Rites)

1058 Babcock, Barbara A., ed. 1978. The Reversible World:
Symbolic Inversion in Art and Society. Ithaca, NY:
Cornell University Press.

1059 Baker, Roger. 1968. Drag: A History of Female Imperson-
ation on the Stage. London: Triton Books.

1060 Cox, Harvey G. 1969. Feast of Fools. New York: Harper
& Row.

1061 Crumrine, N. R. 1969. "Capakoba, the Mayo Easter Ceremonial Impersonator: Explanations of Ritual Clowning."
Journal for the Scientific Study of Religion 8/1:1-22.

1062 Davis, Natalie Zemon. 1973. "The Rites of Violence: Religious Riot in Sixteenth-Century France." Past and Present
59:51-91.

1063 Disher, M. Willson. 1968. Clowns and Pantomimes. New
York: Benjamin Blom.

1064 Doran, John. 1966. The History of Court Fools. New York:
Haskell House.

1065 Frank, J. M. 1977. "Rites of Obscenity: Chariot Songs of
Eastern India." Journal of Popular Culture 10:882-96.

1066 Freedman, J. 1977. "Joking, Affinity and the Exchange of
Ritual Services Among the Kiga of Northern Rwanda: An
Essay on Joking Relationship Theory." Man 12:154-65.

1067 Friedrich, Paul. 1966. "Revolutionary Politics and Communal
Ritual," in Political Anthropology. Ed. Marc J. Swartz
et al. Chicago: Aldine.

1068 Hall, Stuart, and Tony Jefferson, eds. 1976. Resistance
Through Rituals: Youth Subcultures in Post-War Britain.
London: Hutchinson.

1069 Handelman, D. 1976. "Rethinking 'Banana Time': Symbolic
Integration in a Work Setting." Urban Life 4/4:433-48.

1070 _____. 1977. "Play and Ritual: Complementary Frames
of Meta-Communication," in It's a Funny Thing, Humour.
Eds. A. J. Chapman and H. C. Foot. New York: Pergamon Press.

1071 _____. 1981. "The Ritual Clown: Attributes and Affini-
     ties." Anthropos: International Review of Ethnology and
     Linguistics 76/3-4:317-66.

1072 Handelman, Don, and Bruce Kapferer. 1980. "Symbolic
     Types, Meditation and the Transformation of Ritual Con-
     text: Sinhalese Demons and Tewa Clowns." Semiotica
     30/1-2:41-71.

1073 Harris, Monford. 1977. "Purim: The Celebration of Dis-
     order." Judaism 26:161-70.

1074 Jenkins, Ron. 1979. "Becoming a Clown in Bali." The
     Drama Review 23/2:49-56.

1075 Kirby, E. T. 1973. "Mummers' Plays and the Calendar."
     Journal of American Folklore 86:282-85.

1076 Martin, Bernice. 1979. "The Sacralization of Disorder:
     Symbolism in Rock Music." Sociological Analysis 40/2:87-
     124.

1077 Nicoll, Allardyce. 1963. The World of Harlequin: A Criti-
     cal Study of Commedia Dell' Arte. Cambridge, Eng.:
     Cambridge University Press.

1078 Nieburg, H. L. 1970. "Agnostics--Rituals of Conflict."
     Annals of the American Academy of Political and Social
     Science 391:56-73.

1079 Norbeck, Edward. 1963. "African Rituals of Conflict."
     American Anthropologist 65/6:1254-79.

1080 Pearce, Richard. 1970. Stages of the Clown. Carbondale:
     Southern Illinois University Press.

1081 Sarana, Gopala. 1970. "Rituals of Rebellion: The Swazi
     Case Re-Examined." Eastern Anthropologist 23/2:141-62.

1082 Shaw, Peter. 1981. American Patriots and the Rituals of
     Revolution. Cambridge, MA: Harvard University Press.

1083 Syrikin, Alexander. 1982. "On the Behavior of the 'Fool
     for Christ's Sake.'" History of Religions 22/2:150-71.

1084 Willeford, William. 1969. The Fool and His Scepter.
     Evanston, IL: Northwestern University Press.

2.16 RITUAL DRAMA
(Pageants, Experimental Rites,
Entertainment Rites)

1085 Barba, Eugenio. 1979. The Floating Islands. Holstebro,
      Denmark: Thomsens Bogtrykkeri.

1086 Brown, Helen, and Jane Seitz, eds. 1968. "With the Bread
      and Puppet Theatre." The Drama Review 12/2:62-70.

1087 Burkert, Walter. 1966. "Greek Tragedy and Sacrifical Rit-
      ual." Greek, Roman and Byzantine Studies 7:87-121.

1088 Chaillet, N. 1976. "Orghast at Persepolis." Plays and
      Players 24:15-7.

1089 Coult, Tony, and Baz Kershaw, eds. 1983. Engineers of
      the Imagination: The Welfare State Handbook. London:
      Methuen.

1090 Crumrine, N. Ross. 1970. "Ritual Drama and Culture
      Change." Comparative Studies in Society and History
      12/4:361-72.

1091 Crumrine, N. Ross, and M. Louise Crumrine. 1977. "Ritual
      Symbolism in Folk and Ritual Drama of the Mayo Indian San
      Cayetano Velacion, Sonora, Mexico." Journal of American
      Folklore 90/335:8-28.

1092 D'Aponte, Mimi Gisolfi. 1974. "A Passion Play Near Amalfi."
      The Drama Review 18/4:47-55.

1093 De Graft, J. C. 1976. "Roots in African Drama and Thea-
      tre." African Literature Today 8:1-25.

1094 Dickinson, Hugh. 1969. Myth on the Modern Stage. Urbana,
      IL: University of Illinois Press.

1095 Durgnat, Raymond. 1971. "Rock, Rhythm and Dance."
      British Journal of Aesthetics 11/1:28-47.

1096 Ehrensperger, Harold. 1962. Religious Drama. New York:
      Abingdon.

1097 Emigh, John. 1979. "Playing with the Past: Visitation and
      Illusion in the Mask Theatre of Bali." The Drama Review
      23/2:11-36.

1098 Firestone, M. 1978. "Christmas Mumming and Symbolic Inter-
      actionism." Ethos 6/2:92-113.

1099 Flakes, Susan. 1975. "Yoshi and Company." The Drama
      Review 19/4:36-40.

1100 Flanigan, C. Clifford. 1975. "The Liturgical Drama and Its
      Tradition: A Review of Scholarship 1965-1975." Research
      Opportunities in Renaissance Drama 18:81-102.

1101 _____. 1976. "The Liturgical Drama and Its Tradition:
      A Review of Scholarship (Part II)." Research Opportuni-
      ties in Renaissance Drama 19:109-36.

1102 Fletcher, Angus. 1972. The Transcendental Masque.
      Ithaca, NY: Cornell University Press.

1103 Francovich, Allan. 1969. "Genet's Theatre of Possession."
      The Drama Review 14/1:25-45.

1104 Frisbie, Charlotte J., ed. 1980. Southwestern Indian Ritual
      Drama. Albuquerque: University of New Mexico Press.

1105 Gaster, Theodore H. 1977. Thespis: Ritual, Myth, and
      Drama in the Ancient Near East. New York: Norton.

1106 Goethals, Gregor T. 1981. The TV Ritual: Worship at the
      Video Altar. Boston: Beacon.

1107 Gorsky, S. R. 1974. "Ritual Drama: Yeats' Plays for
      Dancers." Modern Drama 17:165-78.

1108 Grimes, Ronald L. 1976. Symbol and Conquest: Public
      Ritual and Drama in Santa Fe, New Mexico. Ithaca, NY:
      Cornell University Press.

1109 _____. 1978. "The Rituals of Walking and Flying: Pub-
      lic Participatory Events at Actor's Lab." The Drama Review
      22/4:77-82.

1110 _____. 1979. "The Actor's Lab: The Ritual Roots of
      Human Action." Canadian Theatre Review 22:9-19.

1111 Grotowski, Jerzy. 1973. "Holiday: The Day That Is Holy."
      The Drama Review 17/2:113-19.

1112 _____. 1978. "The Art of the Beginner." International
      Theatre Information Spring-Summer 7-11.

1113 Halpert, H., and G. M. Story, eds. 1969. Christmas Mum-
      ming in Newfoundland: Essays in Anthropology, Folklore,
      and History. Toronto: University of Toronto Press.

1114 Hardison, O. B., Jr. 1965. Christian Rite and Christian

Drama in the Middle Ages: Essays in the Origin and Early
History of Modern Drama. Baltimore: Johns Hopkins University Press.

1115 Hathorn, Richmond Y. 1962. Tragedy, Myth, and Mystery.
Bloomington, IN: Indiana University Press.

1116 Hawley, John Stratton, and Shrivatsa Goswami. 1981. At
Play with Krishna: Pilgrimage Dramas from Brindavan.
Princeton, NJ: Princeton University Press.

1117 Heilpern, John. 1977. Conference of the Birds: The Story
of Peter Brook in Africa. Harmondsworth, Eng.: Penguin.

1118 Hein, Norvin. 1972. The Miracle Plays of Mathura. New
Haven, CT: Yale University Press.

1119 Hinden, Michael. 1974. "Ritual and Tragic Action: A Synthesis of Current Theory." Journal of Aesthetics and Art
Criticism 32/3:357-73.

1120 Jenkins, L. W., and E. Wapp, Jr. 1976. "Native American
Performance." Drama Review 20:5-12.

1121 Jenkins, R. 1978. "Bali: The Dance Drama Chalonarong."
Drama Review 22:84-8.

1122 Jerstad, Luther G. 1969. Mani-Rimdu: Sherpa Dance-Drama.
Seattle: University of Washington Press.

1123 Johnston, A. F. 1978. "York Cycle: 1977." University
of Toronto Quarterly 48:1-9.

1124 Jones, Clifford R., and Betty True. 1970. Kathakali: An
Introduction to the Dance-Drama of Kerala. New York:
Theatre Arts.

1125 Kallen, Horace Meyer. 1978. The Book of Job as a Greek
Tragedy. Boston: Dynamic Learning.

1126 Keene, Donald. 1966. No: The Classical Theatre of Japan.
Tokyo: Kodansha.

1127 Kirby, E. T. 1974. "Indigenous African Theatre." The
Drama Review 18/4:22-35.

1128 Knowles, D. 1975. "Ritual Theatre: Fernando Arrabal and
the Latin-Americans." Modern Language Review 70:526-38.

1129 Kolankiewicz, Leszek. 1978. On the Road to Active Culture:
The Activities of Grotowski's Theatre Laboratory Institute

in the Years 1970-1977. Trans. Boleslaw Taborski.
Wroclaw, Poland: n. pub.

1130 Kolve, V. 1966. The Play Called "Corpus Christi."
Stanford, CA: Stanford University Press.

1131 Levy, Jerrold E. 1969. "Some Comments upon the Ritual of
the Sanni Demons." Comparative Studies in Society and
History 11/2:217-26.

1132 Lituinoff, Valentina. 1973. "Theatre in the Desert: The
Yaqui Easter." The Drama Review 17/3:52-63.

1133 Mace, Carroll Edward. 1971. Two Spanish-Quiche Dance
Dramas of Rabinal. New Orleans: Tulane.

1134 McLean, Albert F., Jr. 1965. American Vaudeville as Ritual.
Lexington: University of Kentucky Press.

1135 Manning, Frank. 1973. Black Clubs in Bermuda: Ethnography of a Play World. Ithaca, NY: Cornell University
Press.

1136 Mendoza, L. 1977. "Lenten Rites and Practices." Drama
Review 21/3:21-32.

1137 Mennen, Richard. 1976. "Jerzy Grotowski's Paratheatrical
Projects." The Drama Review 19/4:58-69.

1138 Messenger, John C. 1971. "Ibibio Drama." Africa 41:3.

1139 Nicoll, Allardyce. 1963. Masks, Mimes and Miracles. New
York: Cooper Square.

1140 Obeyesekere, Gananath. 1969. "The Ritual Drama of the
Sanni Demons: Collective Representations of Disease in
Ceylon." Comparative Studies in Society and History
11/2:175-216.

1141 _____, and Ranjini Obeyeskere. 1976. "Comic Ritual
Dramas in Sri Lanka." The Drama Review 20/1:5-19.

1142 Peacock, James L. 1968(a). Rites of Modernization: Pro-
letarian Drama as Symbolic Action in Indonesia. Chicago:
University of Chicago Press.

1143 _____. 1968(b). "Ritual, Entertainment, and Modernization: A Javanese Case." Comparative Studies in Society
and History 10/3:328-34.

1144 Roston, Murray. 1968. Biblical Drama in England. Evanston,
IL: Northwestern University Press.

1145 Shank, Theodore. 1974. "A Return to Mayan and Aztec
      Roots." The Drama Review 18/4:56-70.

1146 Soyinka, Wole. 1974. The Bacchae of Euripides: A Com-
      munion Rite. New York: Norton.

1147 Speaight, Robert. 1960. Christian Theatre. New York:
      Hawthorn.

1148 Swann, Darius. 1969. "Indian and Greek Drama: Two
      Definitions." Comparative Drama 3/2:110-19.

1149 Townsen, John. 1974. "Sources in Popular Entertainment."
      The Drama Review 18/1:118-22.

1150 Turner, V. W. 1962. Chihamba the White Spirit: A Ritual
      Drama of the Ndembu. Manchester, Eng.: Manchester
      University Press.

1151 Vickers, Brian. 1973. Towards Greek Tragedy: Drama,
      Myth and Society. Bristol, Eng.: Longman.

1152 Ward, Barbara E. 1979. "Not Merely Players: Drama, Art
      and Ritual in Traditional China." Man 14:18-39.

1153 Warning, Rainer. 1979. "On the Alterity of Medieval Reli-
      gious Drama." New Literary History 10/2:265-92.

1154 Wertz, D. C. 1970. "Doctrines of Confession in English
      Morality Plays." Journal of Religious Thought 27/1:56-62.

1155 Wright, R. 1974. "Community Theatre in Late Medieval East
      Anglia." Theatre Notebook 28/1:24-39.

PART 3. RITUAL DESCRIPTIONS
(Rites of Specific Traditions, Ritual Systems,
Periods, or Geographical Areas)

1156 Agogino, G., and B. Ferguson. 1978. "Easter Ceremony of
the Mayo Indians of Sinaloa, Mexico." Indian Historian
11:17-20.

1157 Aho, J. A. 1977. "Huitzilopochtli's Feast: Sacramental Warfare in Ancient Mexico." Sociological Symposium 18:84-107.

1158 Akire, William H. 1968. "Porpoises and Taro." Ethnology
7/3:280-89.

1159 And, M. 1977. "Mevlana Ceremony." Drama Review 21:83-94.

1160 Ando, Kiichiro. 1960. "On the Extinction of Dozuko Union
and Yashiki-Gami Rite." Japanese Sociological Review
10/1:57-77.

1161 Babb, Lawrence A. 1970. "The Food of the Gods in Clhaltis-
gorph: Some Structural Features of Hindu Ritual." Southwestern Journal of Anthropology 26/3:287-304.

1162 Bartels, L. 1975. "Dabo: A Form of Cooperation Between
Farmers Among the Macha Galla of Ethiopia: Social Aspects,
Songs, and Ritual." Anthropos 70/5-6:882-925.

1163 Barth, Fredril. 1976. Ritual and Knowledge Among the
Baktaman of New Guinea. New Haven, CT: Yale University Press.

1164 Bastide, Roger. 1978. The African Religions of Brazil:
Toward a Sociology of the Interpenetration of Civilizations.
Baltimore: Johns Hopkins University Press.

1165 Black Elk. 1971. The Sacred Pipe: Black Elk's Account of
the Seven Rites of the Oglala Sioux. Ed. Joseph E. Brown.
Baltimore: Penguin.

1166 Boyd, James, and F. M. Kotwal. 1977. "The Zoroastrian
      Paragna Ritual." Journal of Mithraic Studies 2/1:18-52.

1167 Brain, Robert. 1979. Rites Black and White. Ringwood,
      Victoria, Australia: Penguin.

1168 Brock, S. P. 1972. "Studies in the Early History of the
      Syrian Orthodox Baptismal Liturgy." Journal of Theologi-
      cal Studies 23:16-64.

1169 Brown, Joseph Epes. 1978. "Sun Dance: Sacrifice-
      Renewal-Identity." Parabola 3/2:12-15.

1170 Burkert, Walter. 1979. Structure and History in Greek
      Mythology and Ritual. Berkeley: University of California
      Press.

1171 Cabaniss, A. 1954. Amalarius of Metz. North-Holland:
      Amsterdam.

1172 Castile, Rand. 1971. The Way of Tea. Tokyo: Weatherhill.

1173 Chenderlin, Fritz. 1975. "Distributed Observance of the
      Passover: A Hypothesis." Biblica 56/3:369-93.

1174 _____. 1976. "Distributed Observance of the Passover:
      A Preliminary Test of the Hypothesis." Biblica 57/1:1-24.

1175- Christian, William A., Jr. 1972. Person and God in a Span-
1176 ish Valley. New York: Seminar.

1177 Davis, Richard. 1974. "Tolerance and Intolerance of Ambi-
      guity in Northern Thai Myth and Ritual." Ethnology 13/1:
      1-24.

1178 Dentan, Robert K. 1970. "Labels and Rituals in Semai
      Classification." Ethnology 9/1:16-25.

1179 Dickson, K. A. 1971. "Christian and African Traditional
      Ceremonies." Practical Anthropology 18:64-71.

1180 Fallers, L. A., and M. C. Fallers. 1974. "Notes on an Ad-
      vent Ramadan." Journal of the American Adademy of
      Religion 42:35-52.

1181 Firth, Raymond. 1967(a). "The Spirits Depart." New Soci-
      ety 9/241:683-85.

1182 _____. 1967(b). Tikopia Ritual and Belief. Boston:
      Beacon.

1183 _____, and James Spillius. 1963. A Study in Ritual Modi-
     fication: The Work of the Gods in Tikopia in 1929 and 1952.
     London: Royal Anthropological Institute.

1184 Fortescue, A. 1913. The Lesser Eastern Churches. New
     York: AMS Press.

1185 Fought, John. 1969. "Chorti (Mayan) Ceremonial Organiza-
     tion." American Anthropologist 71/3:472-75.

1186 Frisbie, Charlotte J., ed. 1980. Southwestern Indian Ritual
     Drama. Albuquerque: University of New Mexico Press.

1187 Garringries, S. L. 1975. "The Sokagakkai Enshrining Cere-
     mony: Ritual Change in a Japanese Buddhist Sect in Amer-
     ica." The Eastern Anthropologist 28/2:133-46.

1188 Gibbs, P. J. 1978. "Kepele Ritual of the Western Highlands
     of Papua New Guinea." Anthropos 73/3-4:434-48.

1189- Gill, Sam D. 1979. Songs of Life: An Introduction to Nav-
1190 ajo Religious Culture. Leiden: Brill.

1191 Gonda, J. 1980. Vedic Ritual: Non-Solemn Rites. Leiden:
     Brill.

1192 Hanson, P. D. 1973. "Zechariah 9 and the Recapitulation of
     an Ancient Ritual Pattern." Journal of Biblical Literature
     92:37-59.

1193 Haran, Menahem. 1978. Temples and Temple-Service in An-
     cient Israel: An Inquiry into the Character of Cult Phenom-
     ena and the Historical Setting of the Priestly School. Ox-
     ford, Eng.: Oxford University Press.

1194 Harris, Monford. 1976. "Passover Seder: On Entering the
     Order of History." Judaism 25:167-74.

1195 Hickerson, Harold. 1963. "The Sociohistorical Significance
     of Two Chippewa Ceremonials." American Anthropologist
     65/1:67-85.

1196 Howard, James H. 1981. Shawnee!: The Ceremonialism of a
     Native Indian Tribe and Its Cultural Background. Athens:
     Ohio University Press.

1197 Huxley, Francis. 1966. The Invisibles: Voodoo Gods in
     Haiti. New York: McGraw-Hill.

1198 Jackson, A. 1973. "Tibetan Bon Rites in China: A Case of
     Cultural Diffusion." Ethnos 38/1-4:71-92.

1199 _____. 1979. Na-khi Religion: An Analytical Appraisal
       of the Na-khi Ritual Texts. The Hague: Mouton.

1200 Johnston, T. F. 1975. "Ancient Athabascan Ritual in Alas-
       ka." Indian Historian 8:9-25.

1201 Jules-Rosette, B. 1975. African Apostles: Ritual and Con-
       version in the Church of John Maranke. Ithaca, NY:
       Cornell University Press.

1202 Jungmann, J. A. 1951. The Mass of the Roman Rite.
       2 vols. New York: Benziger.

1203 Kapenzi, G. Z. 1974. "Shona and Navaho: A Comparative
       Study of Beliefs and Practices." Missiology 2:489-95.

1204 Kemnitzer, L. S. 1978. "Yuwipi." Indian Historian 11:2-5.

1205 Kennedy, John G., ed. 1981. Nubian Ceremonial Life:
       Studies in Islamic Syncretism and Cultural Change.
       Berkeley: University of California Press.

1206 Kertzer, D. I. 1975. "Participation of Italian Communists
       in Catholic Rituals: A Case Study." Journal for the Sci-
       entific Study of Religion 14:1-11.

1207 Kilson, M. 1970. "Taxonomy and Form in Ga Ritual."
       Journal of Religion in Africa 3/1:45-66.

1208 Kitagawa, Joseph M. 1961. "Ainu Bear Festival (Iyomante)."
       History of Religions 1:95-151.

1209 Kligman, Gail. 1981. Calus: Symbolic Transformation in
       Romanian Ritual. Chicago: University of Chicago Press.

1210 Klostermeier, K. 1974. "Bhaktirasamrtasindhubindu of
       Visvanatha Cakravartin." American Oriental Society Jour-
       nal 94:96-107.

1211 Kraus, Hans-Joachim. 1966. Worship in Israel: A Cultic
       History of the Old Testament. Trans. Geoffrey Buswell.
       Richmond, VA: John Knox Press.

1212 Kumar, Pushpendra. 1974. Sakti Cult in Ancient India.
       Varanasi: Bhartiya.

1213 Lachs, S. T. 1960. "Egyptian Festival in Canticles Rabba."
       Jewish Quarterly Review 51:47-54.

1214 Lambert, W. G. 1968. "Myth and Ritual as Conceived by
       the Babylonians." Journal of Semitic Studies 13:104-12.

1215 Lamphere, Louise. 1969. "Symbolic Elements in Navajo Ritual." Southwestern Journal of Anthropology 25/3:279-305.

1216 Lawler, Michael G. 1980. "Christian Rituals: An Essay in Sacramental Symbolisms." Horizons 7/1:7-35.

1217 Lazarus-Yafeh, Hava. 1978. "Muslim Festivals." Numen 25:52-64.

1218 Leggett, Trevor. 1978. Zen and the Ways. London: Routledge & Kegan Paul.

1219 Lehmann, M. R. 1961. "'Yom Kipper' in Qumran." Revue de Qumran 3:117-24.

1220 Levine, Baruch A. 1974. In the Presence of the Lord: A Study of Cult and Some Cultic Terms in Ancient Israel. Leiden: Brill.

1221 Lewis, Gilbert. 1980. Day of Shining Red: An Essay on Understanding Ritual. Cambridge, Eng.: Cambridge University Press.

1222 Li, Yih-Yuan. 1962. "The Supernatural Concepts and Ritual Behaviors of the Nan-Ao Atayal." Bulletin of the Institute of Ethnology, Academia Sinica 14:1-42.

1223 Lloyd, A. B. 1974. "Religious Ritual at Abydos." Journal of Egyptian Archaeology 60:285-86.

1224 Ludwig, Theodore M. 1974. "The Way of Tea: A Religio-Aesthetic Mode of Life." History of Religions 14/1:28-50.

1225 McCallum, D. Kent. 1965. "The Kunapipi Ritual and Attendant Taboo." Eastern Anthropologist 18/2:80-8.

1226 McEwan, Gilbert J. P. n.d. Priest and Temple in Hellenistic Babylonia. Wiesbaden: Franz Steiner Verlag.

1227 McGrath, T. B. 1973. "Sakau in Towm: Sarawi in Towm." Oceania 44:64-7.

1228 MacMullen, Ramsay. 1981. Paganism in the Roman Empire. New Haven, CT: Yale University Press.

1229 MacRae, G. W. 1960. "Meaning and Evolution of the Feast of Tabernacles." Catholic Biblical Quarterly 22:251-76.

1230 Madigan, Francis Cunningham, and Zenaida N. Rebolos. 1963. "Rituals of the Misamis-Bukidnon Area: A Preliminary Report." Philippine Sociological Review 11/1-2:55-9.

1231 Marwick, M. G. 1968. "Notes on Some Cewa Rituals."
      African Studies 27/1:3-14.

1232 Mends, E. H. 1969. "Some Aspects of Periodic Ritual
      Ceremonies of the Anomaba Fante." Ghana Journal of
      Sociology 5/1:39-48.

1233 Mikalson, J. B. 1976. "Erechtheus and the Panathenaia."
      American Journal of Philology 97:141-53.

1234 Milgrom, Jacob. 1983. Studies in Cultic Theology and Ter-
      minology. Leiden: Brill.

1235 Mitchell, Bonner. 1978. "The SPQR in Two Roman Festivals
      of the Early and Mid-Cinquecento." Sixteenth Century
      Journal 9/4:95-102.

1236 Modi, Jivanji J. 1980. The Religious Ceremonies and Cus-
      toms of the Parsees. New York: Garland.

1237 Morgenstern, Julian. 1966. Rites of Birth, Marriage, Death
      and Kindred Occasions Among the Semites. Chicago:
      Hebrew-Union College.

1238 Muller, Jean-Claude. 1972. "Ritual Marriage, Symbolic
      Fatherhood and Initiation Among the Rukuba, Plateau-
      Benue State, Nigeria." Man 7/2:283-95.

1239 Nadel, S. F. 1970. Nupe Religion. New York: Schocken.

1240 Nebesky-Wojkowitz, Rene de. 1976. Tibetan Religious Dances:
      Tibetan Text and Annotated Translation of the 'Chams Yig.
      The Hague: Mouton.

1241 Newman, Philip L. 1964. "Religious Belief and Ritual in a
      New Guinea Society." American Anthropologist 66/4:257-71.

1242 Olson, Carl. 1977. "Existential, Social, and Cosmic Signifi-
      cance of the Upanayana Rite." Numen 24:152-60.

1243 Ortiz, Alfonso. 1969. The Tewa World: Space, Time, Being
      and Becoming in a Pueblo Society. Chicago: University
      of Chicago Press.

1244 Ortner, Sherry. 1978. The Sherpas Through Their Rituals.
      Cambridge, Eng.: Cambridge University Press.

1245 Ostor, Akos. 1980. The Play of the Gods: Locality, Ideol-
      ogy, Structure and Time in the Festivals of a Bengali Town.
      Chicago: University of Chicago Press.

1246 Ottenberg, Simon. 1975. Masked Rituals of Afikpo: The
      Context of an African Art. Seattle: University of Wash-
      ington Press.

1247 Owen, Gale R. 1981. Rites and Religions of the Anglo-
      Saxons. Totowa, NJ: Barnes and Noble.

1248 Painger, Muriel T. 1971. A Yaqui Easter. Tucson: Uni-
      versity of Arizona Press.

1249 Parke, H. W. 1977. Festivals of the Athenians. Ithaca,
      NY: Cornell University Press.

1250 Patai, Raphael. 1962. "The Ritual Approach to Hebrew-
      African Culture Contact." Jewish Social Studies 24/2:86-96.

1251 Pathirana-Wimaladharma, K. 1973. "Some Observations on
      the Religious Festivals, Village Rituals and the Religiosity
      of the Sinhala Rural Folk in the N.C.P., Ceylon." Social
      Compass 20/2:267-85.

1252 Podet, Allen H. 1976. "Secular Studies and Religious
      Uniqueness: A View of Hanukkah." Religious Education
      71:596-602.

1253 Preston, James J. 1980. Cult of the Goddess: Social and
      Religious Change in a Hindu Temple. New York: Advent
      Books.

1254 Pryke, J. 1966. "Sacraments of Holy Baptism and Holy
      Communion in the Light of the Ritual Washings and Sacred
      Meals at Qumran." Revue de Qumran 5:543-52.

1255 Ray, Benjamin C. 1976. African Religions: Symbol, Ritual,
      and Community. Englewood Cliffs, NJ: Prentice-Hall.

1255a Reichard, Gladys A. 1971. Navaho Religion. Princeton,
      NJ: Princeton University Press.

1256 Reina, R. E. 1962. "Ritual of the Skull in Peten, Guate-
      mala." Expedition 4/4:26-35.

1257 Sangree, Walter H. 1970. "Tribal Ritual, Leadership, and
      the Mortality Rate in Irigwa, Northern Nigeria." South-
      western Journal of Anthropology 26/1:32-9.

1258 Saraswati, Baidyanath. 1977. Brahmanic Ritual Traditions
      in the Crucible of Time. Simla, India: Indian Institute
      of Advanced Study.

1259 Schieffelin, Edward L. 1976. The Sorrow of the Lonely and
      the Burning of the Dancers. New York: St. Martin's.

124   Part 3:   Ritual Descriptions

1260 Scullard, H. H. 1981. Festivals and Ceremonies of the
     Roman Republic. Ithaca, NY: Cornell University Press.

1261 Shiver, Cornelia. 1964. "The Carbonari." Social Science
     39/4:234-41.

1262 Simms, R. M. 1975. "Eleusinia in the Sixth to Fourth Cen-
     turies B.C." Greek, Roman and Byzantine Studies 16:
     269-70.

1263 Singer, Milton, ed. 1966. Krishna: Myths, Rites and Atti-
     tudes. Honolulu: East-West Center.

1264 Stevenson, Margaret S. 1971. The Rites of the Twice-Born.
     1920; rpt. New Delhi Oriental Books.

1265 Stone, Martha. 1975. At the Sign of Midnight: The Con-
     cheros Dance Cult of Mexico. Tucson: University of
     Arizona Press.

1266- Swantz, Marja-Liisa. 1970. Ritual and Symbol in Transition-
1267 al Zaramo Society. Uppsala: Gleerup.

1268 Taft, R. 1975. The Great Entrance. Rome: Pontifical
     Oriental Institute.

1269 Tice, T. N. 1967. "Schleiermacher's Interpretation of
     Christmas: Christmas Eve, the Christian Faith, and the
     Christmas Sermons." Journal of Religion 47:100-26.

1270 Turner, Bryan. 1971. "Belief, Ritual and Experience: The
     Case of Methodism." Social Compass 28/2:187-201.

1271 Turner, V. W. 1961. "Ritual Symbolism, Morality and Social
     Structure Among the Ndembu." Rhodes-Livingston Journal
     30:1-10.

1272 _____. 1962. Chihamba the White Spirit: Ritual Drama
     of the Ndembu. Manchester, Eng.: Manchester University
     Press.

1273 _____. 1967. The Forest of Symbols: Aspects of Ndembu
     Ritual. Ithaca, NY: Cornell University Press.

1274 _____. 1968. The Drums of Affliction: A Study of Reli-
     gious Processes Among the Ndembu of Zambia. Oxford,
     Eng.: Clarendon.

1275 Versnel, H. S. 1976. "Two Types of Roman 'Devotio.'"
     Mnemosyne 29/4:365-410.

1276 Vickery, A. B. 1976. "Holi Celebrations in Kathmandu,
      1974." Folklore 87:220-22.

1277 Vidyarthi, L. P. 1978. The Sacred Complex in Hindu Gaya.
      Delhi: Concept.

1278 Vogt, Evon Z. 1965. "Ceremonial Organization in Zinacan-
      tan." Ethnology 4/1:39-52.

1279 _____. 1976. Tortillas for the Gods: A Symbolic Analy-
      sis of Zinacanteco Rituals. Cambridge, MA: Harvard Uni-
      versity Press.

1280 _____. 1977. "On the Symbolic Meaning of Percussion in
      Zinacanteco Ritual." Journal of Anthropological Research
      33:231-44.

1281 Walker, James R. 1980. Lakota Belief and Ritual. Ed.
      Raymond J. DeMaillie and Elaine A. Jahner. Lincoln:
      University of Nebraska Press.

1282 Wallace, Anthony F. C. 1972. The Death and Rebirth of
      the Seneca. New York: Vintage.

1283 Waters, Frank. 1970. Masked Gods: Navaho and Pueblo
      Ceremonialism. New York: Ballantine.

1284 Wilkinson, John. 1971. Egeria's Travels. London: SPCK.

1285 _____. 1979. "Jewish Influences on the Early Christian
      Rite of Jerusalem." Le Museon 92/3-4:347-59.

1286 Wolf, Arthur P., ed. 1974. Religion and Ritual in Chinese
      Society. Stanford, CA: Stanford University Press.

1287 Wyman, Leland C. 1965. "The Red Antway of the Navaho."
      Sante Fe, NM: Museum of Navajo Ceremonial Art.

1288 _____. 1970. Blessingway. Tucson: University of
      Arizona Press.

1289 _____. 1975. The Mountainway of the Navaho. Tucson:
      University of Arizona Press.

1290 Zelitch, J. 1970. "Lakota Sun Dance." Expedition 13/1:
      19-23.

1291 Zimmerly, D. W. 1978. "When the People Gather." Indian
      Historian 11:40-2.

1292 Zuesse, Evan M. 1980. Ritual Cosmos: The Sanctification of
      Life in African Religions. Athens, OH: Ohio University Press.

PART 4.   GENERAL WORKS IN VARIOUS
FIELD-CLUSTERS

4.1 RELIGIOUS STUDIES, THEOLOGY, ETHICS,
HISTORY OF RELIGIONS

1293 Brandon, S. G. F.   1973.   "Religious Ritual," in Dictionary
of the History of Ideas.   Ed. Philip Wiener.   New York:
Scribners.

1294 Brenneman, Walter L., Jr.   1978.   Spirals: A Study in
Symbol, Myth and Ritual.   Washington, DC: University
Press of America.

1295 Cabaniss, Allen.   1970.   Liturgy and Literature.   University,
AL: University of Alabama Press.

1296 Caillois, Roger.   1960.   Man and the Sacred.   Trans. Meyer
Barash.   Glencoe, IL: Free Press.

1297 Collins, Mary.   1976.   "Ritual Symbols and the Ritual Process:
The Work of Victor W. Turner."   Worship 50:336-46.

1298 Comstock, W. Richard.   1981.   "A Behavioral Approach to
the Sacred: Category Formation in Religious Studies."
Journal of the American Adademy of Religion 49/4:625-43.

1299 De Coppens, Peter Roche.   1977.   The Nature and Use of
Ritual: The Great Christian Documents and Traditional
Blueprints for Human and Spiritual Growth.   Washington,
DC: University Press of America.

1300 Delattre, Roland.   1978.   "Ritual Resourcefulness and Cultural Pluralism."   Soundings 61/3:281-301.

1301 Dixon, John W., Jr.   1973.   "The Metaphoric Transformation:
An Essay on the Physiology of the Imagination."   Sociological Analysis 34/1:56-74.

1302 _____. 1974. "The Erotics of Knowing." Anglican Theological Review 56/1:3-16.

1303 _____. 1977. "Theology and Form: Reflections on the
Spaces of the Imagination." Journal of the American
Adademy of Religion (Supplement) 45/2:593-622.

1304 _____. 1979. The Physiology of Faith: A Theory of
Theological Relativity. New York: Harper & Row.

1305 Doty, William. 1980. "Mythophiles' Dyscrasia: A Comprehensive Definition of Myth." Journal of the American
Adademy of Religion 48/4:531-602.

1306 Driver, Tom F. 1977. Patterns of Grace: Human Experience as Word of God. New York: Harper & Row.

1307 _____. 1981. Christ in a Changing World: Toward an
Ethical Christology. New York: Crossroad.

1308 Dudley, Guilford. 1977. Religion on Trial: Mircea Eliade
and His Critics. Philadelphia: Temple University Press.

1309 Eliade, Mircea. 1954. The Myth of the Eternal Return.
New York: Pantheon.

1310 _____. 1958(a). Patterns in Comparative Religion.
New York: Sheed.

1311 _____. 1958(b). Yoga, Immortality and Freedom.
Princeton, NJ: Princeton University Press.

1312 _____. 1959(a). Cosmos and History. New York:
Harper & Row.

1313 _____. 1959(b). The Sacred and the Profane. New
York: Harcourt.

1314 _____. 1961. Images and Symbols. New York: Sheed.

1315 _____. 1962. The Forge and the Crucible. New York:
Harper & Row.

1316 _____. 1964. Shamanism: Archaic Techniques of Ecstasy.
Princeton, NJ: Princeton University Press.

1317 _____. 1965. Rites and Symbols of Initiation. New
York: Harper & Row.

1318 Elzey, Wayne. 1975. "Liminality and Symbiosis in Popular

Protestantism." Journal of the American Academy of Religion
43/4:741-56.

1319 Frein, G. H. 1972. "Religious Studies as Academic Festivity."
      Council on the Study of Religion Bulletin 3:11-17.

1320 Green, Ronald M. 1979. "Religious Ritual: A Kantian Per-
      spective." The Journal of Religious Ethics 7:229-38.

1321 Grimes, Ronald L. 1976. "Ritual Studies: A Comparative
      Review of Theodor Gaster and Victor Turner." Religious
      Studies Review 2:13-25.

1322 _____. 1979. "Modes of Ritual Necessity." Worship 53/2:
      126-41.

1323 _____. 1982. Beginnings in Ritual Studies. Washington,
      DC: University Press of America.

1324 _____. n.d. "Ritual Studies." Forthcoming in The En-
      cyclopedia of Religion. Ed. Mircea Eliade. New York:
      Free Press.

1325 Hamilton, K., and R. T. Haverluck. 1972. "Laughter and
      Vision." Soundings 55:163-77.

1326 Hardwick, Charley D. 1981. "Elusive Religiosity, Illusions,
      and Truth Telling." Journal of the American Academy
      of Religion 49/4:645-55.

1327 Harrison, Paul. 1977. "Toward a Dramaturgical Interpreta-
      tion of Religion." Sociological Analysis 38/4:389-96.

1328 Harrison, Robert. 1979. "Where Have All the Rituals Gone?"
      in The Imagination of Reality: Essays in South-East Asian
      Coherence Systems. Ed. A. L. Becker and Aram Yengoyan.
      Norwood, NJ: Ablex.

1329 Hatchett, Marion. 1976. Sanctifying Life, Time, and Space:
      An Introduction to Liturgical Study. New York: Seabury.

1330 Hine, Virginia H. 1981. "Self-Generated Ritual: Trend or
      Fad?" Worship 55/5:404-19.

1331 James, E. O. 1973. Christian Myth and Ritual: A Histori-
      cal Study. Gloucester, MA: Peter Smith.

1332 Jennings, Theodore W. 1982. "On Ritual Knowledge."
      History of Religions 62/2:111-27.

1333 Jewett, Robert. 1975. "Religious Studies and Popular Cul-
      ture." Journal of Popular Culture 9:491-2.

1334 Jones, Paul. 1973. Rediscovering Ritual. New York: Paulist.

1335 Kavanagh, Aidan. 1982. Elements of Rite: A Handbook of
Liturgical Style. New York: Pueblo.

1336 Kliever, Lonnie. 1979. "Polysymbolism and Modern Religiosity." Journal of Religion 59:169-94.

1337 _____. 1981. "Fictive Religion: Rhetoric and Play."
Journal of the American Academy of Religion 49/4:658-69.

1338 Lincoln, Bruce. 1977. "Two Notes on Modern Rituals."
Journal of the American Academy of Religion 45/2:147-60.

1339 Miller, David. 1972. Gods and Games: Toward a Theology
of Play. New York: Harper & Row.

1340 Mitchell, Leonel L. 1977. The Meaning of Ritual. New
York: Paulist.

1341 Mitchell, Nathan. 1982. Cult and Controversy: The Worship
of the Eucharist Outside Mass. New York: Pueblo.

1342 Mol, Hans. 1976. Identity and the Sacred. New York:
Free Press.

1343 Moore, Robert, et al. 1983. "Ritual in Human Adaptation."
Zygon 18/3.

1344 Morgan, John H. 1974. "Theology and Symbol: An Anthropological Approach." The Journal of Religious Thought
30/2:51-61.

1345 _____. 1977. "Religion and Culture as Meaning Systems:
A Dialogue Between Geertz and Tillich." Journal of Religion 57:363-75.

1346 _____, ed. 1979. Understanding Religion and Culture:
Anthropological and Theological Perspectives. Washington,
DC: University Press of America.

1347 Neale, Robert E. 1969. In Praise of Play: Toward a Psychology of Religion. New York: Harper & Row.

1348 Panikkar, Raimundo. 1977. "Man as a Ritual Being." Chicago Studies 16:5-28.

1349 Pieper, Josef. 1965. In Tune with the World: A Theory of
Festivity. Trans. Richard and Clara Winston. Chicago:
Franciscan Herald.

1350 Pilgrim, Richard B. 1978. "Ritual," in Introduction to the
      Study of Religion. Ed. T. William Hall. New York: Har-
      per & Row.

1351 Saliers, Don E. 1979. "Liturgy and Ethics: Some New Be-
      ginnings." Journal of Religious Ethics 7/2:173-89.

1352 Schmemann, A. 1963. "Theology and Liturgical Tradition,"
      in Worship in Scripture and Tradition. Ed. Massey Shep-
      herd. Oxford, Eng.: Oxford University Press.

1353 Schmidt, Herman, and David Power, eds. 1977. Liturgy and
      Cultural Religious Traditions. New York: Seabury.

1354 Segal, Robert A. 1980. "The Myth-Ritualist Theory of Reli-
      gion." Journal for the Scientific Study of Religion 19:
      173-85.

1355 Shaughnessy, James D., ed. 1973. The Roots of Ritual.
      Grand Rapids, MI: Eerdmans.

1356 Siirala, Aarne. 1981. The Voice of Illness: A Study in
      Therapy and Prophecy. 2nd ed. New York: Mellen.

1357 Smith, Jonathan Z. 1978. Map Is Not Territory: Studies in
      the History of Religion. Leiden: Brill.

1358 _____. 1982. Imagining Religion: From Babylon to Jones-
      town. Chicago: University of Chicago Press.

1359 Staal, Frits. 1979. "The Meaninglessness of Ritual."
      Numen 26:2-22.

1360 Sullivan, H. Patrick. 1975. "Ritual: Attending to the
      World." Anglican Theological Review (Supplementary Se-
      ries) No. 5:9-32.

1361 Taft, Robert. 1975. The Great Entrance: A History of the
      Transfer of the Gifts and Other Preanaphoral Rites of the
      Liturgy of St. John Chrysostom. Rome: Pontifical Orien-
      tal Institute.

1362 _____. 1978. "The Structural Analysis of Liturgical
      Units: An Essay in Methodology." Worship 52:315-29.

1363 Unterman, Alan. 1980. "The Meaning of Ritual Performance
      in Judaism: Two Basic Structures." Religious Traditions
      3/2:36-52.

1364 Walcott, P. 1979. "Cattle Raiding, Heroic Tradition, and
      Ritual." History of Religions 18:326-51.

1365 Winquist, Charles E. 1983. "Theology, Deconstruction, and
      Ritual Process." Zygon 18/3:295-309.

1366 Worgul, George S. 1980. From Magic to Metaphor: A Vali-
      dation of Christian Sacraments. New York: Paulist.

1367 Zuesse, Evan M. 1975. "Meditation on Ritual." Journal of
      the American Academy of Religion 43/3:517-30.

4.2 ANTHROPOLOGY, ETHNOGRAPHY, ETHOLOGY,
     FOLKLORE, POPULAR CULTURE

1368 Armstrong, Robert Platl. 1971. The Affecting Presence:
      An Essay in Humanistic Anthropology. Urbana: University
      of Illinois Press.

1369 Banton, Michael, ed. 1966. Anthropological Approaches to
      the Study of Religion. London: Tavistock.

1370 Bascom, William. 1970. "The Myth-Ritual Theory." Journal
      of American Folklore 70:103-14.

1371 Bateson, Gregory. 1972. Steps to an Ecology of Mind.
      San Francisco: Chandler.

1372 Beattie, John. 1966. "Ritual and Social Change." Man
      1:60-74.

1373 _____. 1971. "On Understanding Ritual," in Rationality:
      Key Concepts in the Social Sciences. Ed. Bryan R. Wilson.
      New York: Harper & Row.

1374 Beidelman, T. O. 1971. The Translation of Culture: Essays
      to Evans-Pritchard. London: Tavistock.

1375 Boon, James A. 1982. Other Tribes, Other Scribes: Sym-
      bolic Anthropology in the Comparative Study of Cultures,
      Histories, Religions, and Texts. Cambridge, Eng.:
      Cambridge University Press.

1376 Cohen, Abner. 1969. "Political Anthropology: The Analysis
      of the Symbolism of Power Relations." Man (N.S.) 4:213-35.

1377 Corson, S. A., and E. O'Leary Corson. 1980. Ethnology
      and Nonverbal Communication in Mental Health. Oxford,
      Eng.: Pergamon.

1378 Dissanayake, E. 1979. "Ethological View of Ritual and Art
      in Human Evolutionary History." Leonardo 12/1:27-31.

1379 Dolgin, Janet L., et al. 1977. Symbolic Anthropology: A
      Reader in the Study of Symbols and Meanings. New York:
      Columbia University Press.

1380 Douglas, Mary. 1968. "The Contempt of Ritual." New Black-
      friars 49:475-82,528-35.

1381 _____. 1973(a). Natural Symbols: Explorations in Cos-
      mology. New York: Vintage.

1382 _____. 1973(b). Rules and Meanings. Baltimore: Pen-
      guin.

1383 _____. 1978. Implicit Meanings: Essays in Anthropol-
      ogy. London: Routledge & Kegan Paul.

1384 _____, and Baron Isherwood. 1978. The World of Goods:
      Towards an Anthropology of Consumption. New York:
      Norton.

1385 Downs, R. E. 1961. "On the Analysis of Ritual." South-
      western Journal of Anthropology 17/1:75-80.

1386 Durkheim, Emile. 1965. The Elementary Forms of Religious
      Life. Trans. Joseph W. Swain. New York: Free Press.

1387 Fernandez, James W. 1971. "Persuasions and Performances,"
      in Myth, Symbol and Culture. Ed. Clifford Geertz. New
      York: Norton.

1388- _____. 1973. "Analysis of Ritual." Science 182:1366-67.
1389

1390 Geertz, Clifford. 1962. "The Growth of Culture and the
      Evolution of Mind," in Theories of the Mind. Ed. J. Scher.
      New York: Free Press.

1391 _____. 1964. "Ideology as a Cultural System," in Ideology
      and Discontent. Ed. D. Apter. New York: Free Press.

1392 _____. 1966. "Religion as a Cultural System," in Anthro-
      pological Approaches to the Study of Religion. Ed. Michael
      Banton. London: Tavistock.

1393 _____, ed. 1971. Myth, Symbol and Culture. New York:
      Norton.

1394 _____. 1973. The Interpretation of Cultures: Selected
      Essays. New York: Basic Books.

1395 _____. 1975. "Common Sense as a Cultural System."
      The Antioch Review 33/1:5-26.

1396 _____. 1980. "Blurred Genres: The Refiguration of So-
     cial Thought." The American Scholar 49:165-79.

1397 Gluckman, Max, ed. 1962. Essays on the Ritual of Social
     Relations. Manchester, Eng.: Manchester University Press.

1398 _____. 1964. Closed Systems and Open Minds. Edinburgh:
     Oliver & Boyd.

1399 _____, and Fred Eggan. 1965. The Relevance of Models
     for Social Anthropology. London: Tavistock.

1400 Hall, Edward T. 1966. The Hidden Dimension. Garden City,
     NY: Doubleday.

1401 _____. 1973. The Silent Language. Garden City, NY:
     Doubleday.

1402 _____. 1976. Beyond Culture. Garden City, NY:
     Doubleday.

1403 Hill, Carole, ed. 1975. Symbols and Society: Essays on
     Belief Systems in Action. Athens, GA: Southern Anthro-
     pological Society.

1404 Hobsbawm, Eric. 1983. The Invention of Tradition. Cam-
     bridge, Eng.: Cambridge University Press.

1405 Isenberg, Sheldon, and Dennis E. Owen. 1977. "Bodies,
     Natural and Contrived: The Work of Mary Douglas."
     Religious Studies Review 3/1:1-16.

1406 Jensen, Adolf E. 1963. Myth and Cult Among Primitive Peo-
     ples. Chicago: University of Chicago Press.

1407 La Fontaine, J. S., ed. 1972. The Interpretation of Ritual:
     Essays in Honour of A. I. Richards. London: Tavistock.

1408 Leach, Edmund. 1964. "Ritual," in Dictionary of the Social
     Sciences. Ed. J. Gould and W. L. Kolb. London: Tavi-
     stock.

1409 _____. 1968. "Ritual," in International Encyclopedia of
     Social Sciences. Ed. D. L. Sills. Vol. 13. New York:
     Macmillan.

1410 Lessa, William A., and Evon Z. Vogt, eds. 1972. Reader in
     Comparative Religion: An Anthropological Approach. 3rd ed.
     New York: Harper & Row.

1411 Levi-Strauss, Claude. 1963. Totemism. Trans. Rodney
     Needham. Boston: Beacon.

1412 _____. 1966. The Savage Mind. Trans. George Weiden-
     feld and Nicolson, Ltd. Chicago: University of Chicago Press.

1413 _____. 1967. Structural Anthropology. Trans. Claire
     Jacobson and Brooke G. Schoepf. Garden City, NY:
     Doubleday.

1414 Mair, L. 1974. "Ritual and Rationality: Anthropologists on
     Myth." Encounter 43:85-9.

1415 Mead, Margaret. 1966. "Ritual and the Expression of the
     Cosmic Sense." Worship 40/2:67-72.

1416 Middleton, John. 1960. Lugbara Religion: Ritual and Au-
     thority Among an East African People. London: Oxford
     University Press.

1417 _____, ed. 1967. Gods and Rituals: Readings in
     Religious Beliefs and Practices. Garden City, NY: Natural
     History Press.

1418 Myerhoff, Barbara. 1978. Number Our Days. New York:
     Simon and Schuster.

1419 Nagendra, S. P. 1962. "The Nature and Significance of
     Ritual." Eastern Anthropologist 15/1:2-20.

1420 Norbeck, Edward. 1974. "The Anthropological Study of
     Human Play." Rice University Studies 60/3:1-8.

1421 Opler, Morris Edward. 1964. "Particularization and Generali-
     zation as Processes in Ritual and Culture," in Religion in
     South Asia. Ed. E. B. Harper. Seattle: University of
     Washington Press.

1422 Otten, Charlotte M. 1971. Anthropology and Art: Readings
     in Cross-Cultural Aesthetics. New York: Natural History
     Press.

1423 Peacock, James L. 1975. Consciousness and Change: Sym-
     bolic Anthropology in Evolutionary Perspective. New York:
     Wiley.

1424 Pelto, Pertti, and Gretel H. Pelto. 1978. Anthropological
     Research: The Structure of Inquiry. New York: Cam-
     bridge University Press.

1425 Perinbanayagam, R. S. 1974. "The Definition of the Situa-
     tion: An Analysis of the Ethnomethodological and Drama-
     turgical View." The Sociological Quarterly 15/3:521-41.

1426 Rappaport, Roy A. 1971(a). "Ritual, Sanctity, and Cyber-
      netics." American Anthropologist 73:59-76.

1427 _____. 1971(b). "The Sacred in Human Evolution."
      Annual Review of Ecology and Systematics 2:23-44.

1428 _____. 1979. Ecology, Meaning and Religion. Richmond,
      CA: North Atlantic Books.

1429 _____. 1980. "Concluding Remarks on Ritual and Reflex-
      ivity." Semiotica 30/1-2:181-93.

1430 Richardson, Miles. 1980. "The Anthropologist as Word
      Shaman." Anthropology and Humanistic Quarterly 5/4:2.

1431 Saliba, John A. 1976. "Homo Religiosus" in Mircea Eliade:
      An Anthropological Evaluation. Leiden: Brill.

1432 Segal, Robert A. 1983. "Victor Turner's Theory of Ritual."
      Zygon 18/3:327-35.

1433 Senn, H. A. 1977. "Some Werewolf Legends and the Calusari
      Ritual in Romania." Eastern European Quarterly 11:1-14.

1434 Skorupski, John. 1976. Symbol and Theory: A Philosophi-
      cal Study of Theories of Religion in Social Anthropology.
      Cambridge, Eng.: Cambridge University Press.

1435 Spencer, Robert, ed. 1969. Forms of Symbolic Action.
      Seattle: University of Washington Press.

1436 Spradley, James P., ed. 1972. Culture and Cognition:
      Rules, Maps, and Plans. New York: Chandler.

1437 _____, and David W. McCurdy. 1971. The Cultural Ex-
      perience: Ethnography in Complex Society. Chicago:
      Science Research Associates.

1438 Stoeltje, B. J. 1978. "Cultural Frames and Relfections:
      Ritual, Drama, and Spectacle." Current Anthropology
      19:450-51.

1439 Turner, Victor. 1965. "Some Current Trends in the Study
      of Ritual in Africa." Anthropological Quarterly 38/3:155-66.

1440 _____, ed. 1969(a). Forms of Symbolic Action. Seattle:
      University of Washington Press.

1441 _____. 1969(b). The Ritual Process. Chicago: Aldine.

1442 _____. 1974(a). Drama, Fields and Metaphors: Symbolic

Action in a Human Society.   Ithaca, NY: Cornell University
Press.

1443 _____. 1974(b).   "Metaphors of Antistructure in Religious
Culture," in Changing Perspectives in the Scientific Study
of Religion.   Ed. A. Erster.   New York: Wiley.

1444 _____. 1975.   "Ritual as Communication and Potency," in
Symbols and Society: Essays on Belief Systems in Action.
Ed. Carole Hill.   Athens: University of Georgia Press.

1445 _____. 1977(a).   "Process, System, and Symbol: A New
Anthropological Synthesis."   Daedalus 106/3:61-80.

1446 _____. 1977(b).   The Ritual Process: Structure and Anti-
Structure.   Ithaca, NY: Cornell University Press.

1447 _____. 1979.   "Dramatic Ritual/Ritual Drama: Performance
and Reflexive Anthropology."   The Kenyon Review (N.S.)
1/3:80-93.

1448 _____. 1980.   "Social Dramas and Stories About Them."
Critical Inquiry 7/4:141-68.

1449 Wallace, Anthony F. C.   1966(a).   Religion: An Anthropological View.   New York: Random House.

1450 _____. 1966(b).   "Theological Resources From the Social
Sciences: Rituals, Sacred and Profane."   Zygon 1:60-96.

1451 White, Hayden.   1978.   Tropics of Discourse: Essays in Cultural Criticism.   Baltimore: Johns Hopkins University Press.

1452 Wilson, Brian, ed.   1970.   Rationality.   New York: Harper
& Row.

4.3 SOCIOLOGY, SOCIAL PSYCHOLOGY,
POLITICAL SCIENCE

1453 Ahler, James G., and Joseph B. Tamney.   1965.   "Some Functions of Religious Ritual in a Catastrophe."   Sociological
Analysis 25/4:212-30.

1454 Bennett, Lance W.   1980.   "Myth, Ritual and Political Control."   Journal of Communication 30/4:166-79.

1455 Berger, Peter.   1969.   The Sacred Canopy: Elements of a
Sociological Theory of Religion.   Garden City, NY: Doubleday.

1456 Birenbaum, Arnold, and Edward Sagarin, eds. 1973. People in Places: The Sociology of the Familiar. New York: Praeger.

1457 Bloch, Maurice. 1973. "Symbols, Song and Dance: Features of Articulation." European Journal of Sociology 15:55-81.

1458 Blumer, Herbert. 1969. Symbolic Interactionism: Perspective and Method. Englewood Cliffs, NJ: Prentice-Hall.

1459 Bocock, Robert J. 1970. "Ritual: Civic and Religious." British Journal of Sociology 21/3:285-97.

1460 _____. 1974. Ritual in Industrial Society: A Sociological Analysis of Ritualism in Modern England. London: Allen & Unwin.

1461 Canetti, Elias. 1962. Crowds and Power. New York: Viking.

1462 Dawe, A. 1973. "The Underworld View of Erving Goffman." British Journal of Sociology 24:246-53.

1463 Durkheim, Emile. 1965. The Elementary Forms of the Religious Life. Trans. Joseph W. Swain. New York: Free Press.

1464 _____, and M. Mauss. 1963. Primitive Classification. Chicago: University of Chicago Press.

1465 Edelman, Murray. 1964. The Symbolic Uses of Politics. Urbana: University of Illinois Press.

1466 _____. 1971. Politics as Symbolic Action: Mass Arousal and Quiescence. Chicago: Markham.

1467 Fenn, Richard K. 1982. "Recent Studies of Church Decline: The Eclipse of Ritual." Religious Studies Review 8/2:124-28.

1468 Goody, Jack. 1961. "Religion and Ritual: The Definitional Problem.: British Journal of Sociology 12/2:142-64.

1469 Harrison, Paul M. 1977. "Toward a Dramaturgical Interpretation of Religion." Sociological Analysis 38:389-96.

1470 Hesser, Garry, and Andrew Weigert. 1980. "Comparative Dimensions of Liturgy: A Conceptual Framework and Feasibility Application." Sociological Analysis 41/3:215-29.

1471 Lewin, H., and J. Morris. 1977. "Marx's Concept of Fetishism." Science and Society 41:172-90.

1472 Lyman, Stanford, and Marvin Scott. 1975. The Drama of
      Social Reality. New York: Oxford University Press.

1473 Manis, J. G., and B. N. Metzer, eds. 1967. Symbolic Inter-
      action. Boston: Allyn.

1474 Martin, Richard J. 1974. "Cultic Aspects of Sociology: A
      Speculative Essay." British Journal of Sociology 25/1:15-31.

1475 Meddin, J. 1980. "Symbols, Anxiety, and Ritual: A Func-
      tional Interpretation." Qualitative Sociology 3/4:251-71.

1476 Nagendra, S. P. 1970. "Max Weber's Theory of Ritual."
      Indian Journal of Sociology 1/2:173-84.

1477 _____. 1971. The Concept of Ritual in Modern Sociologi-
      cal Theory. New Delhi: Academic Journals of India.

1478 Parsons, Talcott, and Edward Shils, eds. 1952. Toward a
      General Theory of Action. Cambridge, MA: Harvard Uni-
      versity Press.

1479 Pickering, W. S. F. 1974. "Persistence of Rites of Passage:
      Towards an Explanation." British Journal of Sociology
      25:63-78.

1480 Rueckert, William H. 1963. Kenneth Burke and the Drama
      of Human Relations. Minneapolis: University of Minnesota
      Press.

1481 Warner, William Lloyd. 1959. The Living and the Dead: A
      Study of the Symbolic Life of Americans. New Haven, CT:
      Yale University Press.

1482 _____. 1961. Family of God: A Symbolic Study of Chris-
      tian Life in America. New Haven, CT: Yale University
      Press.

4.4 LITERATURE, LITERARY CRITICISM

1483 Altizer, Thomas J. J. 1980. "Ritual and Contemporary Repe-
      tition." Dialog 19:274-80.

1484 Babcock-Abrahams, Barbara. 1974. "The Novel and the
      Carnival World." Modern Language Notes: Comparative
      Literature 89/6:911-37.

1485 Beckson, Karl. 1974. "A Mythology of Aestheticism."
      English Literature in Transition 17:233-49.

1486 Booth, Wayne C. 1974. Modern Dogma and the Rhetoric of
      Assent. Chicago: University of Chicago Press.

1487 Brophy, Robert J. 1973. Robinson Jeffers: Myth, Ritual,
      and Symbol in His Narrative Poems. Cleveland, OH: Case-
      Western.

1488 Burke, Kenneth. 1966. Language as Symbolic Action: Es-
      says on Life, Literature and Method. Berkeley: University
      of California Press.

1489 _____. 1969(a). A Grammar of Motives. Berkeley: Uni-
      versity of California Press.

1490 _____. 1969(b). A Rhetoric of Motives. Berkeley: Uni-
      versity of California Press.

1491 _____. 1970. The Rhetoric of Religion: Studies in Logol-
      ogy. Berkeley: University of California Press.

1492 _____. 1972. Dramatism and Development. Barre, MA:
      Clark University Press.

1493 Cabaniss, Allen. 1970. Liturgy and Literature: Selected
      Essays. University, AL: University of Alabama Press.

1494 Chabrowe, Leonard. 1976. Ritual and Pathos: The Theater
      of O'Neill. Lewisburg, PA: Bucknell University Press.

1495 Coursen, Herbert N., Jr. 1976. Christian Ritual and the
      World of Shakespeare's Tragedies. Lewisburg, PA: Buck-
      nell University Press.

1496 Danahy, Michael. 1973. "The Drama of Herodiade: Liturgy
      and Irony." Modern Language Quarterly 34:292-311.

1497 De Gerenday, Lynn. 1976. "Play, Ritualization and Ambiva-
      lence in Julius Caesar." Literature and Psychology 24:24-33.

1498 Falk, Florence. 1980. "Drama and Ritual Process in A Mid-
      summer Night's Dream." Comparative Drama 14:263-79.

1499 Frye, Northrop. 1968. Anatomy of Criticism. New York:
      Atheneum.

1500 Hardin, Richard F. 1983. "'Ritual' in Recent Criticism: The
      Elusive Sense of Community." PMLA 98/5:846-62.

1501 Hardy, Barbara. 1973. Rituals and Feeling in the Novels of
      George Eliot. Swansea, Wales: University College of Swan-
      sea.

1502 Irwin, John. 1975. Doubling and Incest / Repetition and
      Revenge: A Speculative Reading of Faulkner. Baltimore:
      Johns Hopkins University Press.

1503 Knapp, B. L. 1978. "Dance of Siva: Malraux, Motion and
      Multiplicity." Twentieth Century Literature 24:358-71.

1504 Korb, J. 1979. "Ritual and Experiment in Modern Poetry."
      Journal of Modern Literature 7:127-46.

1505 Lindberg, Henry J. 1974. "James Dickey's Deliverance:
      The Ritual of Art." Southern Literary Journal 6:83-90.

1506 Manlove, C. N. 1979. "The Liturgical Novels of Charles
      Williams." Mosaic 12/4:161-81.

1507 Miller, J. Hillis. 1982. Fiction and Repetition: Seven Eng-
      lish Novels. Cambridge, MA: Harvard University Press.

1508 Myerhoff, Barbara, and Deena Metzger. 1980. "The Journal
      as Activity and Genre: On Listening to the Silent Laughter
      of Mozart." Semiotica 30/1-2:97-114.

1509 O'Reilly, Robert F. 1974. "Ritual, Myth and Symbol in Gide's
      L'Immoraliste." Symposium 28:346-55.

1510 Paulson, Ronald. 1976. "Life as Journey and as Theater:
      Two Eighteenth-Century Narrative Structures." New Lit-
      erary History 8/1:43-58.

1511 Ross, Charles L. 1977. "D. H. Lawrence's Use of Greek
      Tragedy: Euripides and Ritual." D. H. Lawrence Review
      10:1-19.

1512 Rupp, Richard. 1970. Celebration in Postwar Fiction.
      Coral Gables, FL: University of Miami Press.

1513 Simms, Norman. 1975. Ritual and Rhetoric: Intellectual and
      Ceremonial Backgrounds to Middle English Literature. Fol-
      croft, PA: Folcroft.

1514 Stein, Richard L. 1975. The Ritual of Interpretation: The
      Fine Arts as Literature in Ruskin, Rossetti, and Pater.
      Cambridge, MA: Harvard University Press.

1515 Vargo, Edward. 1973. Rainstorms and Fire: Ritual in the
      Novels of John Updike. Port Washington, NY: Kennikat.

1516 Vickery, John B., and J'nan M. Sellery, eds. 1972. The
      Scapegoat: Ritual and Literature. Boston: Houghton
      Mifflin.

1517 Waldhorn, Arthur, and Hilda Waldhorn, eds. 1966. The Rite
      of Becoming: Stories and Studies of Adolescence. New
      York: New American Library.

1518 Weston, Jessie L. 1957. From Ritual to Romance. Garden
      City, NY: Doubleday.

1519 Williams, R. H. 1979. "Critique of the Sampling Plan in
      Shirley Jackson's 'The Lottery.'" Journal of Modern Lit-
      erature 7:543-44.

1520 Zender, Karl F. 1974. "A Hand of Poker: Game and Ritual
      in Faulkner's 'Was.'" Studies in Short Fiction 11:53-60.

                        4.5 PHILOSOPHY

1521 Austin, J. L. 1961. "Performative Utterances," in his
      Philosophical Papers. New York: Oxford University Press.

1522 _____. 1965. How to Do Things with Words. Ed. J. O.
      Urmson. New York: Oxford University Press.

1523 Black, Max. 1962. Models and Metaphors: Studies in Lan-
      guage and Philosophy. Ithaca, NY: Cornell University Press.

1524 Foucault, Michel. 1970. The Order of Things: An Archae-
      ology of the Human Sciences. New York: Random House.

1525 Langer, Susanne K. 1953. Feeling and Form: A Theory of
      Art. New York: Scribner's.

1526 _____. 1957. Philosophy in a New Key: A Study in the
      Symbolism of Reason, Rite and Art. Cambridge, MA: Har-
      vard University Press.

1527 _____, ed. 1961. Reflections on Art. New York: Oxford
      University Press.

1528 _____. 1972. Mind: An Essay on Human Feeling. Balti-
      more: Johns Hopkins University Press.

1529 Morgan, John. 1974. "Religious Myth and Symbol: A Con-
      vergence of Philosophy and Anthropology." Philosophy To-
      day 18/4:68-84.

1530 Morris, Charles. 1938. Foundations of the Theory of Signs.
      Chicago: University of Chicago Press.

1531 Polanyi, Michael, and Harry Prosch. 1976. Meaning.
      Chicago: University of Chicago Press.

1532 Ricoeur, Paul. 1973. "The Model of the Text: Meaningful
      Action Considered as Text." New Literary History 5/1:
      91-117.

1533 Schutz, Alfred, and Thomas Luckmann. 1973. Structures of
      the Life-World. Evanston, IL: Northwestern University
      Press.

1534 Searle, John. 1969. Speech Acts. Cambridge, Eng.:
      Cambridge University Press.

1535 _____. 1975. "A Taxonomy of Illocutionary Acts," in
      Language, Mind and Knowledge. Ed. K. Gunderson.
      Minneapolis: University of Minnesota Press.

4.6 HISTORY, CLASSICS

1536 Ackerman, R. 1975. "Frazer on Myth and Ritual." Journal
      of the History of Ideas 36:115-34.

1537 Angeloglou, Maggie. 1970. A History of Make-up. New
      York: Macmillan.

1538 Deshen, S. 1970. "On Religious Change: The Situational
      Analysis of Symbolic Action." Comparative Studies in So-
      cial History 12:260-74.

1539 Forster, Robert, and Orest A. Ranum, eds. 1982. Ritual,
      Religion, and the Sacred. Baltimore: Johns Hopkins Uni-
      versity Press.

1540 Penner, Hans H. 1968. "Myth and Ritual: A Wasteland or
      a Forest of Symbols?" History and Theory 8:46-57.

1541 Shils, Edward. 1981. Tradition. Chicago: University of
      Chicago Press.

4.7 COMMUNICATIONS, KINESICS,
LINGUISTICS

1542 Benthall, Jonathan, and Ted Polhemus, eds. 1975. The
      Body as a Medium of Expression. New York: Dutton.

1543 Birdwhistell, Ray L. 1970. Kinesics and Context: Essays
      on Body Motion Communication. Philadelphia: University
      of Pennsylvania Press.

1544 Davis, Martha, and Janet Skupien. 1978. Body Movement
      and Nonverbal Communication: An Annotated Bibliography
      1971-1981. Bloomington: Indiana University Press.

1545 Higgins, Joseph R. 1977. Human Movement: An Integrated
      Approach. St. Louis, MO: C. V. Mosby.

1546 Hutchinson, Ann. 1970. Labanotation: The System of Ana-
      lyzing and Recording Movement. New York: Theatre Arts.

1547 Key, Mary R. 1977. Nonverbal Communication: A Research
      Guide and Bibliography. Metuchen, NJ: Scarecrow Press.

1548 Morris, Desmond. 1978. Manwatching: A Field Guide to
      Human Behavior. London: Triad/Granada.

1549 _____, et al. 1981. Gestures: Their Origin and Distribu-
      tion. London: Triad/Granada.

1550 Scheflen, Albert E., and Alice Scheflen. 1972. Body Lan-
      guage and Social Order: Communication as Behavioral Con-
      trol. Englewood Cliffs, NJ: Prentice-Hall.

4.8 PSYCHOLOGY, MEDICINE, BIOLOGY,
PHYSICS, GENETICS

1551 Booth, Gotthard. 1974. The Cancer Epidemic: Shadow of
      the Conquest of Nature. New York: Edwin Mellen Press.

1552 Brown, Judith K. 1978. "Ritual and Gestalt: The Gestalt
      Group in High Relief." Gestalt Journal 1/2:68-74.

1553 Capra, Fritjof. 1975. The Tao of Physics. Boulder, CO:
      Shambala.

1554 Csikszentmihalyi, Mihaly. 1975. Beyond Boredom and Anxi-
      ety. San Francisco: Jossey-Bass.

1555 d'Aquili, Eugene G. 1972. The Biopsychological Determinants
      of Culture. Reading, MA: Addison-Wesley.

1556 _____. 1983. "The Myth-Ritual Complex: A Biogenetic
      Structural Analysis." Zygon 18/3:247-69.

1557 _____, and Charles Laughlin, Jr. 1975. "The Biopsycho-
     logical Determinants of Religious Ritual Behavior." Zygon
     10/1:32-58.

1558 _____, et al. 1979. The Spectrum of Ritual: A Biogene-
     tic Structural Analysis. New York: Columbia University
     Press.

1559 Darwin, Charles. 1965. The Expression of the Emotion in
     Man and Animals. 1872 rpt. Chicago: University of
     Chicago Press.

1560 Ellens, J. H. 1973. "Psychological Dynamics in Christian
     Worship: A Beginning Inquiry." Journal of Psychology
     and Theology 1:10-22.

1561 Erikson, Erik H. 1966. "Ontogeny of Ritualization," in
     Psychoanalysis--A General Psychology: Essays in Honor
     of Heinz Hartman. Ed. R. Lowenstein et al. New York:
     International Universities Press.

1562 _____. 1968. "The Development of Ritualization," in The
     Religious Situation. Ed. Donald R. Cutler. Boston: Bea-
     con.

1563 _____. 1977. Toys and Reasons: Stages in the Ritualiza-
     tion of Experience. New York: Norton.

1564 Freud, Sigmund. 1953. The Standard Edition of the Com-
     plete Psychological Works of Sigmund Freud (SE). Trans.
     James Strachey. 24 vols. London: Hogarth.

1565 _____. 1953. "Totem and Taboo." SE 13:1-161.

1566 _____. 1959. "Obsessive Actions and Religious Practices."
     SE 9:116-27.

1567 _____. 1961. "The Future of An Illusion." SE 21:3-56.

1568 _____. 1964. "Moses and Monotheism." SE 23:3-137.

1569 Gay, Volney P. 1975. "Psychopathology and Ritual: Freud's
     Essay, 'Obsessive Actions and Religious Practices'." The
     Psychoanalytic Review 62:493-507.

1570 _____. 1979. Freud on Ritual: Reconstruction and Cri-
     tique. Missoula, MT: Scholars Press.

1571 _____. 1983. "Ritual and Self-Esteem in Victor Turner
     and Heinz Kohut." Zygon 18/3:271-82.

1572 Georgiades, Thrasybulos. 1983. Music and Language: The
     Rise of Western Music as Exemplified in Settings of the Mass.
     Trans. Marie-Louise Gollner. Cambridge, Eng.: Cambridge
     University Press.

1573 Hillman, James. 1972. The Myth of Analysis: Three Essays
     in Archetypal Psychology. New York: Harper & Row.

1574 _____. 1975. Re-visioning Psychology. New York: Har-
     per & Row.

1575 Jung, C. G. n.d. The Collected Works of C. G. Jung (CW).
     Trans. R. F. C. Hull. Princeton, NJ: Princeton University
     Press.

1576 _____. 1958. "Transformation Symbolism in the Mass," in
     Psyche and Symbol: A Selection from the Writings of C. G.
     Jung. Ed. Violet De Laszlo. Garden City, NY: Doubleday.

1577 _____. 1963(a). "Mysterium Coniunctionis." CW 14.

1578 _____. 1963(b). "Psychology and Religion." CW 11.

1579 _____. 1967. "Symbols of Transformation." CW 2nd. ed.
     5.

1580 _____. 1968(a). "The Archetypes and the Collective Un-
     conscious." CW 2nd. ed. 9/1.

1581 _____. 1968(b). "Aeon: Researches into the Phenomen-
     ology of the Self." CW 9/2.

1582 _____. 1968(c). "Alchemical Studies." CW 13.

1583 _____. 1968(d). "Psychology and Alchemy." CW 12.

1584 Moore, Robert L. 1983. "Contemporary Psychotherapy as
     Ritual Process: An Initial Reconnaissance." Zygon 18/3:
     283-94.

1585 Morton, J. 1972. "Man, the Ritual Animal." Australian and
     New Zealand Journal of Psychiatry 6/2:133-38.

1586 Nehr, Andrew. 1962. "A Physiological Explanation of Unusual
     Behavior in Ceremonies Involving Drums." Human Biology
     34/2:151-60.

1587 Neumann, Erich. 1976. "The Psychological Meaning of Rit-
     ual." Quadrant 9/2:5-34.

1588 Palazzoli, Mara S., et al. 1978. "Family Rituals." Ch. 9 of

their Paradox and Counterparadox: A New Model in the
Therapy of the Family in Schizophrenic Transaction.   New
York: J. Aronson.

1589 Plaut, A.   1975.   "Where Have All the Rituals Gone?   Obser-
      vations on the Transforming Function of Rituals and the
      Proliferation of Psychotherapies."   Journal of Analytical
      Psychology 20/1:3-17.

1590 Posinsky, S. H.   1962.   "Ritual: Neurotic and Social."
      American Image 19:375-90.

1591 Reik, Theodor.   1976.   Ritual: Psychoanalytic Studies.   2nd
      ed.   Trans. Douglas Bryan.   New York: International
      Universities Press.

1592 Sheehy, Gail.   1976.   Passages: Predictable Crises of Adult
      Life.   New York: Bantam.

1593 Turner, Victor.   1983.   "Body, Brain and Culture."   Zygon
      18/3:221-45.

                          4.9   EDUCATION

1594 Bernstein, Basil, et al.   1966.   "Ritual in Education."   Royal
      Society of London: Philosophical Transactions (Series B)
      51/772:429-36.

1595 Burnett, Jaquetta Hill.   1969.   "Ceremony, Rites and Economy
      in the Student System of an American High School."
      Human Organization 28:1-10.

1596 Courtney, Richard.   1974.   Play, Drama and Thought: The
      Intellectual Background to Drama in Education.   2nd rev.
      ed.   New York: Drama Books.

1597 _____.   1980.   The Dramatic Curriculum.   New York:
      Drama Books.

1598 _____.   1982.   Re-Play: Studies of Human Drama in Edu-
      cation.   Toronto: The Ontario Institute for Studies in
      Education Press.

1599 Gehrke, Nathalie.   1979.   "Rituals of the Hidden Curriculum,"
      in Children in Time and Space.   Ed. Kaoru Yamamoto.
      New York: Teachers College Press.

1600 Grumet, Madeleine R.   1978.   "Curriculum as Theatre: Merely
      Players."   Curriculum Inquiry 8/1:37-64.

1601 Kapferer, Judith. 1981. "Socialization and the Symbolic
      Order." Anthropology and Education Quarterly 12/4:258-74.

1602 Lancy, David F. 1975. "The Social Organization of Learning:
      Initiation Rituals and Public Schools." Human Organization
      34/4:371-80.

1603 Levin, David M. 1982. "Moral Education: The Body's Felt
      Sense of Value." Teachers College Record 84/2:283-300.

1604 Olson, Wayne. 1979. "Ceremony as Religious Education."
      Religious Education 74/6:563-69.

4.10 THEATER, ARTS, MUSIC

1605 Appel, Willa. 1969. "The Living Theater and Liminal Ritual."
      Cornell Journal of Social Relations 4/2:69-84.

1606 Artaud, Antonin. 1958. The Theater and Its Double.
      Trans. Mary C. Richards. New York: Grove.

1607 Baker, D. 1977. "African Theatre and the West." Compara-
      tive Drama 11:227-51.

1608 Beck, Julian. 1972. The Life of the Theatre. San Francis-
      co: City Lights.

1609 Belli, Angela. 1969. Ancient Greek Myths and Modern Drama:
      A Study in Continuity. New York: New York University
      Press.

1610 Biner, Pierre. 1972. The Living Theatre. New York:
      Horizon.

1611 Brandon, James. 1974. Theater in Southeast Asia. Cam-
      bridge, MA: Harvard University Press.

1612 Brisset, Dennis, and Charles Edgley. 1975. Life as Theatre:
      A Dramaturgical Sourcebook. Chicago: Aldine.

1613 Brook, Peter. 1968. The Empty Space. New York: Avon.

1614 Burnham, J. 1973. "Contemporary Ritual: A Search for
      Meaning in Post-Historical Times." Arts Magazine 47:38-41.

1615 Burns, Elizabeth. 1972. Theatricality: A Study of Conven-
      tion in the Theatre and in Social Life. New York: Harper
      & Row.

1616 Burzynski, Tadeusz, and Zbigniew Osinski. 1979. Grotow-
      ski's Laboratory. Warsaw: Interpress.

1617 Cetta, Lewis T. 1974. Profane Play Ritual and Jean Genet:
      A Study of His Drama. University, AL: University of
      Alabama Press.

1618 Chaney, David. 1979. Fictions and Ceremonies: Represen-
      tations of Popular Experience. London: Edward Arnold.

1619 Cole, David. 1975. The Theatrical Event: A Mythos, a
      Vocabulary, a Pespective. Middleton, CT: Wesleyan Uni-
      versity Press.

1620 Craig, Gordon. 1925. On the Art of the Theatre. New
      York: Theatre Arts.

1621 Driver, Tom F. 1969. "What We Have to Learn from Antonin
      Artaud." Union Seminary Quarterly Review 25/1:61-73.

1622 Dukore, Bernard F. 1974. Dramatic Theory: The Greeks
      to Grotowski. New York: Holt.

1623 Findlay, Robert. 1980(a). "Grotowski's 'Cultural Explora-
      tions Bordering on Art, Especially Theatre.'" Theatre
      Journal 32:349-56.

1624 _____. 1980(b). "Grotowski's Laboratorium After Twenty
      Years: Theory and Operation." Kansas Quarterly 12/3:
      133-39.

1625 Graham-White, A. 1976. "'Ritual' in Contemporary Theatre
      and Criticism." Educational Theatre Journal 28:318-24.

1626 Grotowski, Jerzy. 1968. Towards a Poor Theater. New
      York: Simon and Schuster.

1627 Hunningher, Benjamin. 1961. The Origin of the Theater.
      New York: Hill and Wang.

1628 Kirby, E. T. 1969. Total Theatre. New York: Dutton.

1629 _____. 1975. Ur Drama: The Origins of Theatre.
      New York: New York University Press.

1630 Meyerhold, Vesevolod. 1969. Meyerhold on Theatre. New
      York: Hill and Wang.

1631 Nicoll, Allardyce. 1966. The Development of the Theatre:
      A Study of Theatrical Art from the Beginnings to the Pres-
      ent Day. 5th ed. rev. New York: Harcourt Brace Jovan-
      ovich.

1632   Ofrat, G. 1979. "Structure of Ritual and Mythos in the
       Naturalistic Plays of August Strindberg." Theater Re-
       search International 4:102-17.

1633   Orenstein, Gloria Feman. 1975. The Theater of the Mar-
       velous: Surrealism and the Contemporary Stage. New
       York: New York University Press.

1634   Pasolli, Robert. 1970. A Book on the Open Theatre. In-
       dianapolis: Bobbs-Merrill.

1635   Pronko, Leonard. 1964. Avant-Garde: The Experimental
       Theater in France. Berkeley: University of California
       Press.

1636   Richmond, Farley. 1971. "Asian Theatre Materials: Se-
       lected Bibliography." The Drama Review 15/3:312-23.

1637   Schechner, Richard. 1973. Environmental Theatre. New
       York: Hawthorn.

1638   _____. 1974. "From Ritual to Theatre and Back: The
       Structure/Process of the Efficacy-Entertainment Dyad."
       Educational Theatre Journal 26:455-81.

1639   _____. 1977. Essays on Performance Theory, 1970-1976.
       New York: Drama Books.

1640   _____. 1981(a). "Performers and Spectators Transported
       and Transformed." The Kenyon Review (N.S.) 3/4:83-113.

1641   _____. 1981(b). "Restoration of Behavior." Studies in
       Visual Communication 7/3:2-45.

1642   _____. 1982(a). "Collective Reflexivity: Restoration of
       Behavior," in A Crack in the Mirror: Reflexive Perspec-
       tives in Anthropology. Ed. Jay Ruby. Philadelphia:
       University of Pennsylvania Press.

1643   _____. 1982(b). The End of Humanism: Writings on
       Performance. New York: Performing Arts Journal Pub.

1644   _____, and Mady Schuman, eds. 1976. Ritual, Play and
       Performance: Readings in the Social Sciences/Theatre.
       New York: Seabury.

1645   Stroup, T. B. 1977. "Ritual and Ceremony in the Drama."
       Comparative Drama 11:139-46.

1646   Weisman, John. 1973. Guerrilla Theatre: Scenarios for
       Revolution. Garden City, NY: Doubleday.

1647 Williams, Raymond. 1968. Drama in Performance. Baltimore:
      Penguin.

1648 _____. 1975. Drama in a Dramatised Society. Cambridge,
      Eng.: Cambridge University Press.

1649 Youngerman, Suzanne. 1978. The Translation of Culture
      into Choreography: Essays in Dance Research. Ed.
      Dianne L. Woodruff. New York: CORD.

AUTHOR INDEX

Ablon, Joan 569
Abrahams, R. D. 389
Achte, Kalle A. 688
Ackerman, R. 1536
Adam, A. 141
Adams, Doug 1, 830, 831
Adedeji, J. A. 909
Adlard, John 621
Agar, Michael 935
Agogino, G. 1156
Aguilar, H. 793
Ahern, Emily M. 390
Ahler, James G. 1453
Aho, J. A. 1157
Akire, William H. 1158
Albanese, Catherine 936
Albrecht, Ruth 261
Aldrich, M. R. 937
Alenikoff, F. 2
Allmen, J. J. 65
Altizer, Thomas J. J. 1483
Ames, Michael M. 191
Anant, Victor 689
And, M. 1159
Ando, Kiichiro 1160
Andreasen, N. E. 142, 622
Andronikof, C. 832
Angeloglou, Maggie 1537
Anglo, S. 714
Appadurai, Arjun 715
Appel, Willa 1605
Apte, Usham 540
Ardener, Shirley 67
Aries, P. 541, 570, 571
Armstrong, L. 3
Armstrong, Robert Platl 1368
Arno, A. 716
Arnold, I. R. 623

Artaud, Antonin 1606
Austin, J. L. 1521, 1522
Awolalu, J. O. 690, 794
Azouf, Mona 624

Bartels, L. 1162
Babaeva, R. 542
Babb, Lawrence A. 625, 1161
Babcock, Barbara A. 224, 315,
   1058
Babcock-Abrahams, Barbara
   1484
Bachelard, Gaston 68
Baer, R. A., Jr. 833
Bahr, Donald M. 938
Baker, D. 1607
Baker, Roger 1059
Ballinger, Franchot 69
Bandem, I. M. 4
Banton, Michael 1369
Barba, Eugenio 1085
Barfield, Owen 1007
Barker, G. 763
Barnes, A. J. 143
Barry, H. 520
Barth, F. H. 543
Barth, Fredrik 1163
Bascom, William 1370
Bastide, Roger 1164
Bateson, Gregory 1371
Bateson, Mary Catherine 834,
   1008
Bauman, R. 389
Bauman, Richard 391
Bayer, Raymond 5
Beane, W. C. 144
Beattie, John 262, 1372, 1373

151